ADDIE JOSS

KING OF THE PITCHERS

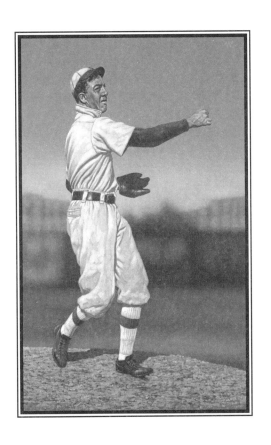

ADDIE JOSS

KING OF THE PITCHERS

Scott Longert

Acknowledgments

My sincere thanks to many members of the extended Addie Joss family for their invaluable assistance in providing clippings, photos, anecdotes, and scrapbooks, which went a long way in making this work a reality. Thanks also to Jeanne Dornfeldt of Family Tree Research, for her skills in uncovering details regarding Jacob Joss and the early days in Juneau.

I am deeply grateful to Bob Broeg for his generous foreword.

Thank you to SABR for helping me get this manuscript out on the playing field.

A very special thanks to my wife Vicki for her love, patience, and positive attitude, which kept me on track when times were lean and rejection notices plentiful. Finally, thanks to the tall skinny kid from a small midwestern town who showed me what courage, determination, and plenty of heart could do to make one's dreams come true. Though it didn't hurt to have a pretty good fastball, either.

Contents

Forward

Bob Broeg

HMM, THE WORD "JOSS" STANDS FOR "GOD" IN CHINESE, and that really isn't a bad introduction for Addie Joss, one of the best baseball pitchers, long gone, but fortunately brought to life through the tender research and writing of Scott Longert. As a sports writer, even an ancient one, I ought to be especially proud because Addie was one of us: an off-season newspaper bloke whose efforts were good enough that he could have made a career writing about the game in whose efforts he made history. You see, even if you haven't guessed it by now Joss was one of the best ever at throwing a baseball, good enough to qualify for John McGraw's 30-year capitulation of the game as a ranking manager and authority.

When Joss died in April, 1911, just two days after his thirty-first birthday, he was young enough to establish quantity with his quality, but it was his excellence just short of 10 years that captivated many baseball scholars and just pure fans, who badgered the National Baseball Hall of Fame for a waiver that would permit Addie's induction. Mostly, I'll take only a slight assist on that one. Joining the Hall of Fame's Committee on Veterans in 1972, a young pup in the mid-50's among graying giants of the game, I asked chairman Warren Giles to clarify a rule. Hall of Fame restrictions required participation in "ten championship seasons." Did that mean he had to be a 10-year man? No, it didn't in the wisdom of Mr. Giles.

So I quickly pointed out that I'd listened to Hall of Fame members of the Hall of Fame committee (Bill Terry, Frank Frisch and Ford Frick, to name three) extol the virtues of Ross (Pep) Youngs, McGraw's pet as a hustling, versatile outfielder with the champion New York Giants of the early 1920's. Youngs, described by Frisch as "Enos Slaughter with even more ability," died after playing 95 games into his tenth season, 1927. When Youngs was quickly elected, why not Joss, even more qualified? As noted in dramatic detail by author Longert, Addie had fallen deathly ill just before his last tune-up previous to opening the 1911 season, his tenth. The answer was happily answered in 1978 when the Hall of Fame board of directors certified dear Addie as eligible.

So the man who pitched probably the most significant game in baseball history received the honest honor, richly deserved in the judgment of those who had the good fortune to see him and to those of us who didn't, though fortunate enough now to have Longert cap research about the rangy righthander. Joss had an incredible won-and-lost percentage (.623), the second-lowest earned-run average in baseball history (1.88), and (to repeat) was the man who pitched the most significant game.

Want to argue? Okay. But just as two well-deserved Hall of Fame pitchers, Christy Mathewson early and Jim Palmer late, lost their biggest game, Adrian Joss won his. Bone-weary Matty lost the famed Merkle boner replay to Chicago in 1908 and Pancakes Palmer pancaked in Baltimore's final-day bid to overtake Milwaukee in 1982.

Just think of the situation when Joss toed the slab the final weekend of the 1908 season when four clubs (even the St. Louis Browns!) went down to the wire with a championship chance, and Addie was opposed to baseball's hottest and winningest pitcher. The Chicago White Sox's Big Ed Walsh went 40-15 that year with an ERA almost as low as Joss' league leading figure. Yeah, and

Big Ed, who it is said could strut sitting down, allowed only four hits and one unearned run.

As mentioned at the outset of this petit-four preamble to Scott Longert's rich dessert of things big and little about Joss, the lower-cased joss is defined by the Chinese as a "god" and an "idol." And in plain old Anglo-Saxon a legend if only because Joss kept Cleveland in contention with a game. The only other no-reach effort that comes close was Don Larsen's spotlighted World Series accomplishment in 1956. Larsen pitched then a no-windup motion, regarded as revolutionary. Thanks to Longert's research, we know that Joss pitched with a wicked sidearm delivery and an ability to hide the ball from a batter. With overpowering stuff, Addie also had the pinpoint control of a Greg Maddux.

I knew a little about Addie Joss (talked to Ty Cobb about him under a silvery Cooperstown moon a couple of years before Ty died in 1961) but I learned more, a lot more in the detailed digging done by this book's author.

As the "elongated twirler," to use the cliché of Joss's day, Joss ranked in the company of Walter Johnson in the critical view of Cobb, who appreciated that Addie was a fifth infielder who could take away many things, including the bunt. As noted in the interesting account of an All-Star team of major leaguers, gathered to pay tribute to the fallen warrior with a benefit game, Cobb was both a contributor and a performer. And if you're not impressed too much about the nearly $14,000 raised by baseball for Joss's wife and children, please be reminded that the amount almost a century ago would be nearly a quarter-million dollars now.

If there's an economist in the house who wants to challenge my relative estimation of the financial impact then and now, be my guest, but do read on about Addie Joss, the Swiss whiz from Wisconsin.

Scott Longert has done about Joss what most certainly Addie as one of the greatest pitchers never would have allowed. The author has hit a literary home run about the best sportswriting ball player ever.

Addie circa 1890.

From Child to Ballplayer

THERE WERE MORE PEOPLE MILLING AROUND the downtown streets of Juneau, Wisconsin than folks had ever remembered seeing. A steady stream of buggies, wagons, and families on foot slowly congregated near Oak Grove and Main Streets. Although it was a weekday afternoon, many businesses displayed "Closed" signs on their front doors. Few shopkeepers expected to do any business that day. The mob of townspeople continued on their way to City Park, laughing and talking excitedly about the day's scheduled event. They hadn't come to see a band concert, or speeches to commemorate some historical happening. Everyone in town put aside their daily responsibilities for the chance to see a tall, lanky, teenager throw a baseball at incredible speed. They all came to see him, proud that one of their own could whip any town team within fifty miles. All eyes were glued on the smiling young pitcher taking his warm up tosses near the home team bench. He zipped the ball sidearm, getting stunning velocity out of the long right arm that seemed to reach his knee. Everybody in the park knew they were about to see pitching at its best.

Adrian Joss was born April 12, 1880 in Woodland, Wisconsin, the only child of Jacob and Theresa Joss. A native of Switzerland, the elder Joss emigrated to Wisconsin during the Civil War era. Aware of the inexpensive government land available, Jacob's parents sent him across the ocean to learn the cheese-making trade. With the abundance of unspoiled grazing land and clear streams, opportunities for novices in the dairy industry knew no bounds. By 1870, 1.5 million pounds of cheese were produced in Wisconsin, much of it shipped abroad to England.

Jacob amassed a fortune making cheese, building his own factory and buying up no fewer than eleven pieces of land in Woodland. On one of these parcels he built a home, settling there in December, 1876, with his new bride, twenty-year-old Theresa Staudenmayer. A tall woman with pleasant features, the educated Mrs. Joss had the capacity to converse on a wide variety of subjects, from politics to baseball. She complemented her husband, who developed a keen interest in local politics. An imposing man, standing well over six feet tall, Jacob sported a thick black goatee to match his flashing dark eyes and wavy hair. He wore a long black suit coat, enhancing his already commanding figure. Within several years he had pushed his way to the forefront of the local Republican party.

Entering politics was nothing out of the ordinary for a man related by marriage to the Staudenmayers. Theresa's father, John G. Staudenmayer, served as town chairman of Caledonia, Wisconsin. A native of Wurtemberg, Germany, John G. had taken the advice of a friend, left army service in his homeland, and headed for America. While Germans of wealth and means settled in the larger cities of Milwaukee and St. Louis, John G. opted for Portage, Wisconsin where much government land remained for the taking. The trip took him seven weeks by ship, train, and stagecoach, and he arrived in Portage carrying only $2 and a letter of introduction from his doctor friend. Through sheer hard work, John G. earned enough money to buy his own property. Within several years he owned 160 acres of prime land.

Refusing to align himself with any political party, John G. promoted the best interests of his constituents. He served on the

County Board of Supervisors, and in later life was appointed by the great reformer, Governor Robert LaFollette, to a state commission on water rights and irrigation. An unselfish and caring man, John G. passed these traits on to his eldest daughter, Theresa. Under trying circumstances, she succeeded in instilling these virtues in John G.'s first grandchild, Addie.

As a young boy, Addie began attending school in the township of Herman. He studied lessons with his Aunt Elizabeth, who had recently arrived from Switzerland. Elizabeth spoke no English, relying on six-year-old Addie to help her with the new language. Both aunt and nephew benefited from the arrangement. Elizabeth learned to speak without an accent, and Addie eventually became a teacher.

The Joss's fortunes turned downward within a decade. Jacob lost a bid for assemblyman in 1884. Three years later he sold all of his Woodland property and accepted a political appointment as deputy sheriff of rural Dodge County. When the Josses arrived in Juneau, the population stood at 500. Jacob quickly impressed the locals with his zeal. One winter's day, the Juneau *Telephone* dispatched a reporter to follow him on his official duties. The writer filed a colorful story. "On Wednesday last we made a flying trip to Horicon, and the term flying is used in a literal sense too, as we rode across the country with Sheriff Joss, whose little ponies seemed to bound through the snow drifts with the speed of antelopes. We thought that Jake was either 'showing off' or trying to reduce the Democratic vote, by impaling us on a barbed wire fence or braining us against a fence post, but he assured us that he had struck his subpoenaing gait: all for the sake of the overburdened taxpayers and the honor of reform."

But after only a year, the elections of 1888 swept the Republicans out of the sheriff's office, and Jacob's fortunes declined further. He became a town constable, and then worked part-time for the volunteer fire department before breaking down completely in September, 1890. He died on Friday October 6, 1890, age thirty-seven, of liver disease.

A Juneau *Telephone* editorial frankly stated the cause of Jacob's death as alcoholism, held his life up as an example of the evils of drink, and chastised him posthumously for being too free with his money and leaving his family in dire straits. Addie grew up knowing that his father had been a kind and capable man, but also that he had been unable to tame his demons and had watched his business and his family's secure future evaporate. It's no wonder that Addie the ballplayer fought hard for a decent payday and thought carefully about his career after baseball.

No will had been recorded, so Theresa petitioned the probate court to recover any assets left behind. It became apparent that the bulk of Jacob's fortune had been exhausted. Theresa soon rented space in Juneau's business district, opening a small millinery shop and sewing school. A skilled seamstress and dressmaker, she correctly assessed the need for a local store that specialized in ladies' hats. Theresa hired her labor cheaply, recruiting Addie to run various errands after school and weekends. After several months of labor, Addie sauntered into the shop, announcing he no longer desired employment. Asked why he had come to that decision, Addie stated emphatically, "Well, Guy never has to do anything at home." Addie, quite naturally, had become envious of his close friend Guy Taft, who like a number of the boys in town had time to play horseshoes and croquet after school. Theresa quietly explained to her employee that his situation was a bit different from that of the other boys.

Work, however, seldom got in the way of baseball. Relatives recall him rarely going anywhere without a baseball clutched tightly in his right hand. As a boy he was considerably taller than his peers. Early photographs show him as a collection of arms and legs, a glimpse of the large frame he was destined to grow into. During his vacation time, Addie traveled to Caledonia to visit his mother's family. In between pickup games, he volunteered to work on the farms, and he was often asked to carry water to the fields. Sometimes Addie would disappear, but thirsty workers knew they could find him by looking skyward over the cornstalks to spot a small white sphere rising and falling against the blue sky.

The first inkling of Addie's baseball prowess occurred on the farm of his aunt and uncle, William and Sophie McLeish. After unsuccessful efforts to round up sides for a game, Addie resigned himself to practice throwing against the side wall of the farmhouse. Alone and undisturbed, he began cutting loose with a velocity unheard of for a boy his age. Within moments Addie startled himself by caving in a brick on the well-built structure. Unsure what reaction to expect, Addie walked slowly to the door and confessed to his aunt and uncle what he had done. The McLeishes were astounded, but not angry. Word of Addie's throwing power spread, and relatives and neighbors stopped by to take a peek at the wall, which the McLeishes did not repair, the better to celebrate their nephew's powerful right arm. (The brick has recently been replaced, but family members still know the exact spot where the legend of Addie Joss began).

The highlight of every summer in Juneau was the Dodge County Fair. Addie and friends virtually lived at the fairgrounds, taking in all the sights and sounds the festive occasion had to offer. Theresa Joss delighted in relating the story of the opening day of the County Fair. Addie was wandering around the fairgrounds enjoying himself when he heard several men discussing a major issue. The Juneau nine was a man short for their afternoon ball game. They needed of a substitute or the game would be forfeited. Addie dropped his lemonade and raced for home. He arrived breathless at the door and asked his startled mother to get his lunch ready quick. "Our team is short a man and I think I can play in his place," Addie gasped excitedly. There is no record of the results of the contest, but it is safe to assume Juneau did not forfeit.

By the time Addie reached high school, he towered over his classmates. He was tall, skinny, and raw-boned, with unusually long arms. By all accounts, he had inherited his father's kind demeanor, which became one of his most endearing qualities. His warm, friendly, smile charmed people from the moment they met him. All his life, he had a genuine talent for putting people at ease. In line with his aspirations of becoming a teacher, he was a good student, attending class regularly and keeping up with his daily assignments.

Theresa Joss had taken on the responsibility of raising a young boy alone, and had produced a fine young man. She had endured much and worked hard, all for her son. She was clearly little interested in her career as a milliner or in the town Juneau except as means to her end of bringing Addie up as well as she could. When Addie signed a contract to play baseball in Cleveland, Theresa quietly closed her shop, packed her possessions and moved back to Portage.

Addie's first venture into organized sports was football. As a senior at Juneau High School, he played right tackle, opening up gaping holes for halfbacks like John "Roxy" Walther, a gifted athlete in his own right, to sprint through. Juneau captured the county championship, outscoring their four opponents, 92-0. Their fourth and final game matched them against rival Mayville, located twelve miles away. An ugly mix of rain and snow dampened the boys' enthusiasm to make the trip, but Mayville officials phoned Juneau, warning the school if the boys were not on the playing field by the two o'clock starting time, the game would be forfeited. A wagon was quickly dispatched, arriving at the playing field moments before the deadline. Juneau came away victorious, 28-0. When the team returned to Juneau the proud community turned out to greet them, presenting the boys with a silk pennant. It was Addie's first athletic triumph.

Addie tasted his first sample of organized baseball in the spring of 1896. He played second base for the high school team, while Roxy Walther pitched. The Juneau nine had a mediocre season, leaving behind no box scores to track statistical accomplishments. A *Telephone* article did mention his fielding against Beaver Dam High: "Addie Joss at second and Stanley Pettibone at short stop took care of the pigskin every time it came into their territory." This was Addie's first mention in print as a ballplayer.

At graduation ceremonies on June 25, 1896, Addie offered an oration on General Nathaniel Greene, entitled "A Hero of the Revolution." With their class motto, "More Beyond," the five 1896 graduates of Juneau High School took their places in the small community. Addie followed through on his teaching plans, studying for and passing the examination to obtain his certificate. He began what he thought would be his career the following September in nearby Horicon—a homecoming of sorts, because his birthplace of Woodland lay within the township.

To enter the teaching profession at the age of sixteen posed numerous challenges. The positions available were usually in small towns and villages, and the teacher had to sink or swim without any assistance. A new instructor was paid in the neighborhood of four to five hundred dollars—not much even a century ago. But for Addie, there was one great benefit. He had the summer off to play ball.

Addie joined the town team in 1897, and his first appearance as a pitcher came against neighboring Beaver Dam. Staked five runs to work with in the early innings, Addie breezed to his first win. He overpowered the Beaver Dam hitters, striking out fourteen, while allowing one base on balls. After another easy win Addie and his teammates decided to take to the road, challenging the northern resort town of Fox Lake. Here they met a veteran team that had played together for years. What Juneau lacked in experience they made up for in effort. Trailing 6-2, they launched a comeback, scoring five runs. Addie couldn't hold the lead, though, and he allowed three runs as Fox Lake prevailed, 9-7. The home team came away impressed with the visitors display. The Fox Lake *Representative* astutely said of the game, "Joss was in the box for Juneau and pitched a very clever game for a seventeen-year-old, striking out seven men and holding the boys down to eight hits. He is a comer and will make a ball player with a little more seasoning."

Baseball season over, Addie journeyed to Herman to prepare for the fall term. There is no date recorded, but at some point during the semester, a gentleman named Edwin P. Brown paid a visit to the young schoolmaster. Brown taught English and coached baseball at the Wayland Academy, situated in Beaver Dam. He had seen Addie pitch, and he wanted to secure his services for spring, 1898. In those unregulated days, schools and universities openly, hired outsiders to represent their athletic teams, though some were a bit more discreet than others. Newspapers commented on this mercenary practice, and for the most part endorsed it. (Wayland and its hired pitcher would discover that opposing schools were represented mostly by players who had finished their educations years before. The academy was hardly in a position to complain.)

What inducements were offered to Addie are unknown, but after the spring term in Herman, Addie traveled directly to Beaver Dam and registered at Wayland. Wayland Academy was affiliated with the University of Chicago, and offered Dodge County students the equivalent of a college degree. Here Addie received his first real coaching. He developed an assortment of pitches to complement his overpowering fastball. A sharp curve became one of his staples, and he mastered a change of pace that had batters falling all over themselves. To further confound hitters, Addie developed the unique windup that was to become his trademark in later years. Standing straight up, he rested his arms just below his waist. He would then rock on his left foot, while turning his right foot clockwise. Taking a full windup, he raised his arms completely above his head, while turning his body to face second base. Beginning his delivery plateward, Addie kicked his left leg high into the air while hiding the baseball behind his thigh until the last possible instant. While driving his body forward, he launched the ball sidearm. Exercising great balance, he finished in an upright position, feet square, ready to field any ball hit near the mound. Batters, particularly righthanders, had difficulty picking up the ball. Many likened his delivery to a tangle of arms and legs with the ball shooting out from somewhere in between. Like most young pitchers, Addie struggled to master control. His early box

Addie and Theresa in 1892, after Jacob's death.

scores indicate ample bases on balls, which gradually decreased by the time he entered the American League.

Addie's initial appearance for Wayland resulted in a loss to his alma mater, Juneau High School, 7-5. With scores of friends in attendance, Addie struck out nine, but gave up a ton of hits to boys two years younger. After the inauspicious debut, he got his first win against the Fox Lake club, 18-8. On Memorial Day, Wayland scheduled a game against Beaver Dam, which was graciously permitted to field the team of its choice. To guarantee a fine holiday crowd, all businesses were asked to close at one o'clock. A gate was set up to charge a fee to enter the grounds: gentlemen twenty five cents, ladies and children fifteen. All proceeds from the contest went toward fixing up the ballfield. The large crowd circling the playing field had a positive effect on Addie. He proceeded to pitch his first shutout, fanning twelve men as Wayland romped to a 25-0 win. The Dodge County *Citizen* lauded the performance, saying, "The imperturbable Joss chewed gum and quietly sent his opponents out in one, two, three order."

The spring schedule concluded with Addie winning two more games to bring his record to seven wins against two losses. His performance at the bat was solid. He hit .325 and stole twelve bases. The deal with Wayland Academy paid off for both parties. The school gained an impressive baseball season, and their pitcher got coaching and the chance to hone his skills in an organized environment.

Free for the summer, Addie rejoined the Juneau nine to find a much more ambitious schedule laid out by the club's backers. The upcoming Sunday afternoons were filled with games against Sacred Heart Academy, Watertown, and Waupun, which featured Roxy Walther and a young catcher named John "Pete" Kleinow. At the tail end of the schedule loomed the dreaded Jefferson Blues.

The Juneau officials knew they had a star in the making in Addie. Their opponents enjoyed more talent and resources, but none possessed a pitcher with the ability to match Joss. He was the great equalizer, letting his small town mix it up with the big boys. The Juneau *Telephone* got swept up in the excitement, devoting several columns a week to game summaries. Broadsides were printed to announce the time and location of each contest. This was classic, old-fashioned town baseball at its best. The locals bragged all week in the saloons and barbershops, boasting to all that their team was invincible. Wagering ran emotions even higher, and loud, boisterous crowds turned out at the local ballpark.

After an unimpressive 9-5 win over Watertown, Juneau entertained Hartford, the visitors from Washington County. Addie pitched a remarkable game, striking out nineteen and giving up just two hits. To close out the season, Hartford made a return visit with similar results. Addie faced thirty batters, not allowing a single base hit. In an eleven-inning loss to the Jefferson Blues, he struck out fifteen. His teammates committed six errors and allowed five unearned runs. Despite several such tough losses, the season was a great success. Pitching against strong competition, Addie proved himself to be one of the top hurlers in the state. He had boosted Juneau's status to heights never before achieved. The *Telephone* boasted patriotically, "No power on earth is barred from our gates. We may engage in spirited contests and even suffer occasional defeats, but no foe can fire across our bow and achieve a Dewey victory."

As September rolled around, Addie prepared to teach another term of school, but before he reported to the classroom, he received a visit from officials representing Sacred Heart College in Watertown. For considerations including tuition and board, he agreed to pitch for the school team the following spring. This presented a great opportunity, both athletically and academically. With little hesitation, Addie sent his resignation to the Dodge County School Board. He never taught again.

Baseball had started informally at Sacred Heart, but by the late 1890s the administration had resolved to assemble a first class team that could compete with any club in Wisconsin. Officials from the school embarked upon an ambitious journey to seek out the best ballplayers in the state. Other top quality players the college recruited were catcher John "Pete" Kleinow and Addie's old teammate, Roxy Walther, who had settled at shortstop. The roster was potent

Sacred Heart opened the 1899 season on a blustery April 16 at Delafield, against St. John's Military Academy. In front of five hundred curious spectators, Sacred Heart took a 1-0 lead into the bottom of the fourth. With nobody out, St. John's loaded the bases on a hit and a pair of walks. Addie handled his first crisis with relative ease, striking out the side. Sacred Heart went on to win, 4-1. Addie wowed the crowd with thirteen strikeouts. St. John's only run came in on a throwing error.

The next weekend the Jefferson Blues came to Watertown for

a much-anticipated contest. The Sunday game brought a huge crowd to Washington Park. In the early going Addie displayed a bout of wildness—or control. Feelings ran deep between the communities. Jefferson had bitterly protested Sacred Heart's player acquisitions. The Watertown newspaper in return took great offense at the accusations, defending the practice: "The Jefferson *Banner* in its write-up at the ball game between Sacred Heart and the local team of that city finds fault and says our players are picked up from all over the state and most of the players are paid. We are surprised to see such an item in a paper edited by a man who has always had an interest in baseball. He, as well as everyone else, knows that players in the larger cities are hired and no kick is registered by anyone."

It may well be that throwing at hitters was the agreed upon response to the unpopular accusation. In any event, before Addie began throwing strikes, three Jefferson batters limped to first base with welts on their legs. In the top of the fourth, Sacred Heart scored nine runs, the highlight being Addie's home run to deep left field. The final score was Sacred Heart 18, Jefferson 3. Watertown rooters filed out of the park shaking their heads in wonder. They had expected to see a struggle of titans, not the one-sided pounding dished out by Joss and company.

After two straight shutouts with a combined twenty-one strikeouts, Addie and his teammates began to receive statewide attention. The Milwaukee *Journal* wrote a complimentary piece about the college ball club. "Out at Watertown they have a baseball team that bids fair to be shifted to Milwaukee before the season ends if the boys continue the early season's pace. It is the Sacred Heart College team, with an outside battery and the way they are eating up all the amateur teams they are meeting is a caution to dyspepsia. Nobody pretends to do any business out there these days when there is a baseball game on. The residents can hardly finish their dinners in time to get out for the preliminary practice."

The *Journal* gave an accurate assessment of the goings on in

Watertown. Plans were already underway to sign the entire Sacred Heart roster to represent the city on the semipro circuit. Once the college schedule reached its conclusion, Addie would change uniforms to pitch for the Watertown club. All the college players agreed to do the same, insuring the city of a banner summer of baseball.

The spring season finished with a game against Ripon College, scheduled, in honor of Addie, in Juneau. In a truly festive atmosphere, 1,000 people turned out to see Addie pitch the season finale. Most realized that this would be their last chance to watch their hometown star perform at home. Delighted with the crowd of family and friends, Addie dazzled the spectators, striking out thirteen and pitching his fourth shutout of the year. His record for the college season showed eight wins in nine starts. Sacred Heart claimed the mythical Wisconsin college championship of 1899. No other college in the state offered a challenge.

Stories about Addie often state that he attended the University of Wisconsin—even that he was a graduate. Even the hometown Juneau *Telephone*, in his obituary, reported that Addie had enrolled at Wisconsin, only to drop out when he discovered he would not be allowed to compete for the University's team because he had lost his amateur status. The local newspaper's claim to especially solid information is clouded, though, by its assertion in the same article that Addie had prepared for a career as a lawyer. He studied civil engineering at Sacred Heart, and never mentioned any interest in the law. Wisconsin has no record of Addie enrolling at any branch of the university, and there is no evidence that he attended any school after 1899.

While the backers of the Watertown club built a grandstand and fenced in the grounds, the players prepared themselves for an ambitious summer schedule. The day Charles Comiskey brought his Western League St. Paul professionals, local fans were in a frenzy. Some of the visiting team had National League experience, while the remainder were up-and-comers. In two years, Comiskey's team would enter the upstart American League as the Chicago

White Sox. For two innings, Addie pitched flawless baseball against the professionals, holding them hitless while Watertown pushed across three runs. The advantage quickly dissipated when St. Paul's left fielder blasted a grand slam home run. Before the slaughter concluded, Addie was shelled for nine runs as the big boys demonstrated why they were operating near the game's highest level.

But baseball men were taking note of the tall young fastballer in the Wisconsin woods. Shortly after the St. Paul defeat, Connie Mack came calling. Mack, after an undistinguished major league career as a catcher, now owned and managed the Milwaukee franchise of the Western League. He offered Addie a contract to play for Albany, New York. Assurances were given stating if he made good there, a promotion to Milwaukee would occur. The prospect of leaving Wisconsin for the foreign land of New York, did not sit well with Addie. He informed Mack that Albany was out of the question, but that he would enjoy a move direct to Milwaukee. The

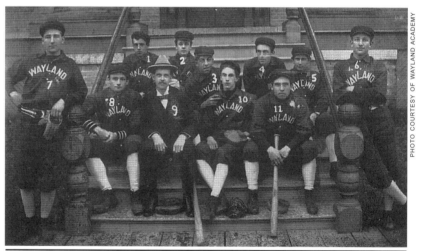

The Wayland Academy squad of 1896. 1. Burt Shepard; 2. John Price; 3. Addie Joss; 4. Winfield Smart; 5. George Rasmussen; 6. Harmon McIntyre; 7. E. L. McIntyre; 8. Earl Wells; 9. E. P. Brown; 10. Russell Moris; 11. John Schwendener.

two men could not come to an agreement, and Mack left town empty handed, but he kept tabs on Addie for the rest of the summer.

Mack's interest made Addie ponder his worth on the market, and he began looking around for a better financial situation. When the Oshkosh Indians offered him $10 a week, he jumped the Watertown club without a backward glance, leaving them in the lurch and creating an unpleasant situation among his former teammates and friends. To complicate matters further, his first start for Oshkosh came against his old club. The game summary in the Watertown *Times* put it all in perspective. It read, "Joss, who formerly pitched for the home team, was in the box for the visitors and was batted all over the field. The crowd guyed the pitcher unmercifully, and he was retired at the end of the fifth inning.".

Settling in Oshkosh, Addie quickly realized that all was not well with the Indians. Fan interest was low. The local newspaper pronounced baseball dead in Oshkosh, calling for the team to disband. With such overwhelming support the owners soon found themselves in a major financial crisis. A succession of postponements due to bad weather emptied the pockets of management. They reluctantly announced to the players a temporary freeze on salaries. This caused Addie to erupt in anger, and he refused to pitch another game until he got paid. No doubt some of his frustration came from his hasty decision to leave Watertown for what had seemed to be greener pastures. Addie stuck to his guns, steadfastly refusing to play without pay. Facing certain financial ruin, the owners forked over $10 to pay Addie for the weekend. Hours before Addie's scheduled start, a massive thunderstorm roared through Oshkosh, washing away any chance of getting the contest underway. The hapless owners promptly disbanded the team.

Stuck in an unfamiliar city, Addie found himself unemployed and out of funds. A new Oshkosh team was put together, whose owners wanted Addie to play second base. Unhappy but broke, he reluctantly accompanied the team on an eastern trip to Manitowoc. While Oshkosh took a pounding, Addie quietly inquired of the home team's management if they could use a good pitcher. They could.

In its next game, Manitowoc showcased its newest hurler against Appleton. A large crowd gathered to see what the kid from Juneau could do. Addie put on a dazzling exhibition of pitching, leading Manitowoc to a hard fought victory. The Manitowoc *Daily Herald* wrote, "Considerable interest centered about Joss, Manitowoc's new find, and in the game of yesterday he proved a 'poor' josh for the Appleton boys. He had speed to burn and kept them guessing at every stage." The switch to Manitowoc didn't just free Addie from the horrors of Oshkosh, it led him to his first professional contract.

While pitching against Sheboygan later in the season, Addie faced a power hitting third baseman named Bert Schills, who was being scouted by professional clubs. Schills lived up to his reputation, planting one of Addie's fast balls high over the left field fence. At the season's close, he was offered a contract to play for the Toledo Mud Hens of the Inter-State league. The contract included a note which asked if he could recommend any good pitchers. Schills eagerly signed the contract, and advised the Toledo owner to send a contract to Juneau, in care of Addie Joss. Several months later, Addie picked up a letter at the post office from the Toledo Mud Hens Baseball Club. To his astonishment, a contract calling for seventy five dollars a month—if he made the team—was included. The scouting system at the turn of the century centered more on luck than organized evaluation. Many bodies invited to spring training increased the chance of finding a quality ballplayer.

Pride of the Mud Hens

ON MARCH 30, ADDIE BADE FAREWELL to friends and neighbors, and boarded a train for the long ride to Toledo. The Mud Hens already had a staff of proven pitchers. Addie knew he had little time and only a few opportunities to show Toledo manager Bob Gilks his stuff. The intense competition, mixed in with a touch of homesickness, weighed heavily on Addie's broad shoulders. He had no friends or family to lean on for support. To survive this test he called upon all the inner strength and courage he could muster.

Arriving in Toledo, Addie reported to Charles Strobel, who had purchased the Mud Hens in July, 1896, winning a championship in his initial season. Strobel had many interests outside of baseball, the most prominent being a financial stake in the embryonic field of aviation. He poured considerable sums of money into hot air balloon expeditions, promoting the ventures as the future means of transportation in the United States. Possibly the thought of a cheaper method of travel for his ballplayers occurred to him. In between aviation experiments, Strobel could be found in the local band room, conducting marching bands. A skilled bandmaster, Strobel often led the parades in celebration of opening day at the ballpark.

Early spring weather in Ohio produced few days suitable for practicing baseball. Most of the time was spent indoors, running laps and going through a variety of calisthenics. On April 17, Addie made his professional debut, catching several innings against the Detroit Tigers who were passing through town on their way home from spring training. Six days later Addie got the call to pitch against the Columbus Giants, a touring Negro league team. With Gilks scrutinizing every move, Addie overcame a case of the jitters beating the Giants, 4-2. Gilks, an old baseball man, noticed Addie's ability to pitch in the clutch and recognized a star on the rise. He congratulated Addie on making the team, then advised him to rest up to pitch the opening game against Mansfield, Ohio.

The Inter-State league of 1900 boasted of eight franchises in the circuit. Ohio led the way with five representatives, Columbus, Dayton, Mansfield, Youngstown, and Toledo. The remaining three teams were scattered around the Midwest: Fort Wayne, Indiana; New Castle, Pennsylvania; and the Stogies from Wheeling, West Virginia. The league began regular season play on April 28.

The Mud Hens thrilled an opening day crowd of three thousand, by defeating Mansfield, 16-8. Addie staggered through the game, holding on for dear life as his teammates committed six errors. In spite of the sloppy play, all in attendance were visibly impressed with the new pitcher. One fan in particular asked for an introduction as soon as possible. Two years later Lillian Shinavar became Mrs. Adrian Joss.

Addie's first season in Toledo produced nineteen victories against sixteen losses. He pitched several memorable games, one of which generated a nickname that would stick throughout the years. After posting a three-hit shut out against Wheeling, the Toledo *Bee* reported, "Elongated Twirler shut the Wheeling aggregation out. Addie Joss was the Poo-bah at Armory Park yesterday. In nine innings he held the Wheeling team down to three hits, and no runs, and allowed no Stogie to get beyond second base. The game was the best seen on Armory Park for some time."

Addie returned to Toledo in the spring of 1901, to find himself pitching in the Western Association. The franchises of Mansfield, Youngstown, Wheeling, and New Castle, were all victims of an ambitious expansion plan by the remaining owners. The men in charge believed that adding larger cities to the circuit would generate bigger crowds and higher revenues. They awarded franchises to Louisville, Kentucky, Grand Rapids, Michigan and Marion and Indianapolis, Indiana. Charles Strobel built a new section of bleachers in Armory Park.

On May 1, Addie got his first start against Marion. He pitched poorly, allowing eight runs in a losing effort. Six days later he recorded his initial win of the season, once again giving up eight runs in a 9-8 slugfest. Over the next two weeks, Addie righted himself, pitching strongly throughout the month. However the support behind him was nonexistent, resulting in three straight 2-1 losses. Rumors began to surface that the reason for the Mud Hens lousy start centered on certain players hanging around the saloons at all hours. Annoyed by the accusations, Strobel released a statement to the newspapers that if anyone could bring him proof of his ballplayers drinking, he would pay $50 reward. Whether any money did get paid out went unrecorded.

As summer arrived in northwest Ohio, Addie's pitching arm heated up. After a 4-2 victory over Dayton, the Toledo *Bee* wrote, "The game was a pretty exhibition of pitching skill and Joss simply played with the opposing batters after the first inning. In Joss, Strobel has undoubtedly the best pitcher in the league. As a rule the team fails to hit behind him, and he has more close wins and losses than any man on the team."

Addie began to draw the attention of major league clubs. The Boston Americans offered $1,500 for his contract. Within days the St. Louis Cardinals matched the Boston bid. Strobel received a wire from Arlie Latham, a former major league player and an umpire in the Western Association. Latham represented an anonymous buyer who wanted Strobel to give him a price for the rights to Addie. Strobel announced to all parties that his pitcher was not for sale at the present time.

Addie as a Toledo Mud Hen.

Sensing that a shot at the fast company loomed ahead, Addie just kept pitching. He reached the twenty-win plateau by early September, beating Columbus, 4-0, while allowing four singles and contributing a two-run homer. Four days later he stopped Dayton on one hit, coasting to a 7-1 victory. In his final start of the season, he struck out thirteen to register his twenty-seventh win of the year.

Addie dominated the 1901 Western Association. He struck out a total of 210 in 370 innings. He recorded four shutouts while walking only sixty-seven. Addie accounted for more than a third of Toledo's victories.

With the regular season finished, Addie boarded a train destined for Racine, Wisconsin. Located in the southeastern part of the state, Racine had challenged Appleton, its northern rivals, to a one-game playoff for the unofficial state championship. Interest in the game ran high, and the Racine newspaper predicted that a crowd of four thousand would appear on game day. To make things interesting, fans from both sides wagered heavily on the outcome. With Addie striking out fourteen, including eight in a row, Racine won easily, 13-4. Stung by the humiliating defeat, the Appleton players demanded a rematch. Both sides agreed to meet one week later in Racine. The results were much the same. Racine won handily, 6-2. Addie fanned ten batters in front of an estimated five thousand spectators who, in early October, had still not gotten enough baseball.

While the Racine players celebrated, representatives from Kenosha arrived to fling down the gauntlet. They proposed an October 20 contest to determine the absolute baseball championship of Wisconsin. Confident that Addie could not be beaten, Racine accepted. Kenosha signed Chicago's eccentric Rube Waddell, who promised to feed Racine hitters a steady dose of sizzling fastballs. Rumors flew that Kenosha had also signed players from the Milwaukee Brewers. The Racine newspapers estimated that thousands of dollars would change hands on Sunday afternoon, setting the stage for an emotion-packed struggle.

Hours before game time, an excursion train chugged slowly

into Racine. The train carried twelve cars completely filled with fervent Kenosha fans already worked up to fever pitch. They paraded through the streets, ringing cow bells and blowing horns. The mob squeezed into Athletic park, where estimates ranged between five and eight thousand totally crazed spectators.

Addie trotted to the mound amidst a deafening roar from hometown rooters. He had pitched in Ft. Wayne, Dayton, and Louisville, but he had never experienced as wild a crowd as this one. Eager to bring home a win, he worked quickly, setting down the side in order. Waddell showed why he was a major league hurler, striking out the side in the bottom half of the inning. With two out in the top of the second, Kenosha managed to put two runners on base. This brought Waddell, a good hitting pitcher to the plate. Addie studied his opponent, unsure of what pitches the Rube could handle. He threw a fastball, which Waddell drove to deep left field. Before the ball could be retrieved, two runs scored on the stand-up triple. Addie managed to keep his composure, noticing Rube edging a bit too far from third. He took a quick wind up, zipping the ball home as Waddell broke for the plate. Rube was tagged out by the catcher to end the inning.

Trailing by two runs, Addie demonstrated to the massive crowd why he'd won twenty-seven games that season for the Mud Hens. He throttled the Kenosha batters, slamming the door the rest of the way. Waddell matched the performance, striking out the first nine hitters he faced. In the bottom of the fourth, Racine pushed across its first run without the benefit of a base hit. A walk, stolen base, and an error set up the tally on a long sacrifice fly. In the fifth, Racine tied the game on a single, two stolen bases and a throwing error.

The hometown fans sensed a shift in momentum. Addie continued to set down the Kenosha hitters, while Waddell displayed a touch of wildness. A sixth inning walk and stolen base set up the go-ahead run. When the ninth inning finally came around, the fans geared themselves up for a gut-wrenching climax. Addie faltered with two outs, surrendering back-to-back singles before

Waddell strode to the plate, determined to repeat his second inning heroics. In the center of a deafening vortex of sound, Addie calmly reached back for something extra, fanning Waddell on three straight pitches. Racine claimed the championship 4-2. Pandemonium reigned. Delirious rooters dashed en masse out of the grandstand, hoisted Addie on their collective shoulders, and carried him around the park on a jubilant victory lap. The Kenosha fans silently trudged out of the park, unnoticed by the celebrants on the field.

The clash between Racine and Kenosha became a mythical event as the years rolled by. It was probably the greatest semipro game ever staged in Wisconsin, and one of the greatest played anywhere. As for the two pitchers, their paths would cross again in the very near future.

Addie returned to Juneau intent upon resting his long right arm. But days after his arrival he answered a pounding at his front door. There stood a group of boys from the nearby town of Clyman, which had one ballgame left on its schedule. Tom Godsell, the spokesman for the group, explained they had been soundly whipped once by a Watertown team and wanted to square the series tomorrow. Would Addie help them out? The boys may have reminded him of a skinny sixteen-year-old kid struggling to get people out for the old Juneau nine. Having already pitched 397 innings during the summer, he agreed to pitch for the boys the next day.

Tom Godsell had assured Addie the Watertown players wouldn't recognize him because he had been away for several years. A few moments before game time, Addie approached the field in Clyman, wearing farm clothes and work boots. Indeed, the Watertown players had no idea who the tall righthander was. The game moved along swiftly, with Clyman in the lead. Godsell, who served as the team's catcher, swelled with pride at his own ability to handle Addie's pitches. He began to dream about a real future as a player. How many catchers in Dodge County, he reason to himself, could handle the great Addie Joss's fastball?

Late in the game, Watertown produced an unexpected rally, loading the bases with nobody out. Addie motioned to his young catcher to join him on the mound for a quick conference. Godsell jogged out from behind the plate, anxious to hear the strategy planned. He detected a change in Addie's expression, which up until the moment had reflected an easy demeanor. Addie said, "Say kid, we're in a bad spot. I'm going to have to burn them in for a while. You put your mitt where you want the ball and it'll be there."

The realization that Addie had been toying with the young batters hit Tom Godsell squarely on the shin guards. One glance at Addie's face let him know that from now out the fun and games were over. He jogged back to the plate knowing he was about to learn a lesson. Addie wound up and unleashed a sidearm rocket that nearly knocked Godsell off his feet. He feared his left hand had broken. Two more similar offerings had the catcher on his knees, hugging the ground for balance. Somehow he made it through the inning, his left hand numb and throbbing. The shocked Watertown players realized something was rotten in Clyman. They had never seen such speed. The Clyman boys broke out in fits of laughter, and revealed the identity of their ringer. Tom Godsell examined his raw left hand in awe. When his swollen palm and fingers returned to normal, he would enjoy a good laugh and savor the story for years to come.

Addie returned to Juneau, his thoughts turning to more serious matters. Soon the letters and telegrams from major league teams would be piling up on his doorstep. He had little faith in Mud Hens owner Strobel, who displayed no indication that he was willing to sell his best pitcher's contract to a big league club. Probably waiting for top dollar, Strobel was effectively blocking Addie's advancement to the majors, much as Jack Dunn blocked Lefty Grove's a generation later. But in the atmosphere created by the war between the old-line National League and the upstart American League, players could often make moves that would have been impossible a few years before and would become impossible again a few years in the future. One way or another, Addie Joss was going to be a major league pitcher.

The Human Slat

DURING THE FALL OF 1901, word immediately began circulating that Addie had signed a contract to play ball for Brooklyn of the National League. Owner Charles Ebbets had visited a number of Mud Hens, convincing them he had obtained their releases from Charles Strobel. Several players signed contracts. Strobel immediately announced that no releases had been given, and the players repudiated their National League contracts. Addie's name was not among those affected, but Ebbets continued to try to lure him to Brooklyn, offering an automobile and a resort vacation.

Toledo manager Bob Gilks knew the bidding war between the two major leagues was heating up, and he understood that, contract or no contract, his star pitcher might be swept away if Strobel didn't take direct action to secure his services for another year. He urged his boss to go to Juneau personally and persuade Addie to come back to Toledo, where they could protect him from the predators of the major leagues and talk him around to remaining with the Mud Hens. Strobel agreed, and wired Addie to expect him in Juneau for a visit. In mid-January Strobel arrived in town, agreeing to meet at the U.B.B. club, a gathering spot for the young lions of Juneau and a Joss hang-out, for a series of contract negotiations. The two sat down for several lengthy, but inconclusive, discussions. Strobel tried to persuade Addie to be his guest in Toledo for several weeks, but Addie declined the offer, saying only that he might come down and visit after Easter. The negotiations caused quite a stir in Juneau, which rarely saw any visitors of note in the dead of winter. Much of the town ventured out to catch a glimpse of Strobel, who clearly enjoyed the attention.

In an interview with local reporters, the Toledo owner said, "I am positive that Joss will wear a Toledo uniform the coming season. I could not, under any consideration afford to let him go from my claim list, as he is a great favorite with base ball fans in Toledo. I am congratulating myself on being confident of securing his services." Unknown to the reporters or anyone else, Strobel had given Addie a $150 advance for his services the next spring, but he departed Juneau without a signed player's contract.

Just days away from the start of spring training, Cleveland manager Bill Armour reviewed his pitching prospects for the upcoming season. Armour, recently hired away from Dayton of the Western Association, felt that he needed one more strong arm to solidify his team and was well aware of Joss's talent. He huddled with team executives Charles Somers and Jack Kilfoyl, and the three men decided, in the spirit of the times, to go after Addie, despite the fact that he technically belonged to Toledo.

Armour bought a train ticket for Juneau, registering at the local hotel as J.J. Jackson, traveling salesman. Armour casually made inquiries that led him to Addie, and presented the young pitcher with his proposition. He assured Addie that the Cleveland club would protect him from the inevitable legal difficulties with Strobel, and produced a brand new $500 bill as a signing bonus. Addie knew Armour fairly well from his two years in Toledo. The manager had already brought in several players from the Western Association, and if he joined Cleveland he would have some familiar faces around. Cleveland was also a "western" city, much more accessible to home and to his sweetheart in Toledo than, say, Brooklyn. And there was that bonus. Addie signed a contract to play baseball for the Cleveland Bluebirds, and the following morning the two confederates slipped out of town for the long trip to New Orleans.

Despite all his precautions, Armour's secret mission became public virtually overnight. Somehow word leaked out to several newspapers, including the Pittsburgh *Leader*. The paper claimed to have an eyewitness account of the signing who provided the following description. "Joss seemed in no hurry to do business when Armour first approached him, but the instant the $500 Willie was flashed all was changed. The pitcher gasped, rubbed his eyes, then wildly clutched at the bill with his left hand, grabbed a pen with his right and in a cracked voice ordered Armour to produce the contract." The account is colorful but it is unlikely that anybody witnessed the transaction. Besides, Addie may not have seen a $500 bill before, but he had begun to make good money. Pitching post-season games for Racine paid quite well, usually in silver dollars.

Several days later an attorney representing the Toledo Mud Hens appeared in Juneau, seeking a court date for a hearing. The lawyer contended that Addie had signed a contract to play for Toledo and therefore still belonged to Charles Strobel. He requested the courts to set a trial date as soon as possible. The attorney may as well have traveled to Juneau, Alaska, for his chances of receiving a trial date were remote at best. The community strongly supported its home grown pitcher. The docket conveniently showed no open dates.

The Juneau *Telephone* reported the Toledo contract was a conditional one, in which the only agreement called for Addie to receive a certain sum of money if he won a certain number of games. This constituted a gambling contract, one which was not considered legally binding under the law. The Mud Hens lawyer recognized he had little chance of pursuing the case. He returned to Toledo advising Strobel to let go of his claim. Strobel announced to the Toledo papers his decision to release Addie Joss from his reserve list. He asserted there were a half dozen pitchers in camp who could pick up the slack. He had lost not only his best pitcher, but the sum a big league team would have paid him for his contract.

Spring training of 1902 brought hope and anticipation to those who followed the fortunes of the untested Cleveland Bluebirds. Their maiden season of 1901 had produced a seventh-place finish in the eight-team American League, which owners Somers and Kilfoyl deemed unacceptable. They had hired Armour for his experience in bringing along young talent as he had done at Dayton. When he arrived in New Orleans with Addie in tow, Somers beamed with pleasure. Sportswriters sent a steady stream of optimistic reports home to Cleveland, where fans waited patiently for their ballclub to return home and renew past glories.

Cleveland was a city with a long baseball tradition dating back some thirty-three years to the formation of the Cleveland Forest Citys. A respected amateur aggregation, the club chose to turn professional to challenge the mighty Cincinnati Red Stockings. Two contests produced lopsided losses of 25-6 and 43-20. Undaunted by the overwhelming defeats, Cleveland pressed on, becoming a charter member of the National Association of Baseball Players, the game's first organized professional league. Cleveland owners, anxious to cash in on the new venture, offered season tickets at the bargain price of six dollars. The package included parking privileges along the first and third base lines that allowed gentlemen to drive their carriages directly on the field and remain comfortably seated inside.

For over twenty years the Cleveland franchise wallowed in mediocrity. In 1891, then owner Frank DeHaas Robison built a brand new ballpark to accommodate the anticipated crowds eager to support a winning team. League Park was constructed at the intersection of Dunham and Lexington Avenues, where Robison's trolley lines delivered fans right to the front gate. Acquiring the likes of Cy Young, Jesse Burkett, and catcher Chief Zimmer, Cleveland captured the Temple Cup in 1895, defeating the Baltimore Orioles. Seemingly on the brink of a dynasty, the franchise quickly unraveled under the pressure of Robison's business dealings. In 1899, he transferred its best players to St. Louis, a franchise he also owned, and the Cleveland club, then known as the Spiders, went 20-134, for what remains the worst record in the history of major league baseball. Major league baseball disappeared from Cleveland after that season.

Unknown to disheartened Cleveland fans, Ban Johnson, president of the Western League, was working to create a new major league, designed specifically to compete with the long established National. Fortunately for the Cleveland faithful, Johnson saw Cleveland as a vital link in a circuit that originally involved Chicago, Milwaukee, Detroit, Boston, Philadelphia, Washington, and Baltimore. In 1900 Johnson pitched his idea to young, wealthy Charles Somers. Somers sought out the aid of his friend, clothing store magnate Jack Kilfoyl. Industrialist Joseph Hook Somers, Charles's father and the founder of the family fortune, tried to dissuade his son from associating with baseball, fearful that the family business would fall into disarray. Young Somers's socialite wife feared baseball would ruin their marriage. She pleaded with "Charley" to stay away from baseball for the sake of herself and their young daughter. Deaf to the pleas of his family, Somers accepted Johnson's proposal to become the owner of the Cleveland entry into the American League. He put up most of the money and, typically, appointed himself vice-president. Kilfoyl would serve as the club's president.

While the new owners set about building a baseball team, Johnson returned to Cleveland for a conference. The new league had money problems. Fellow owners Connie Mack in Philadelphia and Charles Comiskey in Milwaukee didn't have enough money to build ballparks, while the Boston franchise still had no ownership at all and was being run by the league. Somers made loans to Mack and Comiskey, and established a six-figure line of credit with a Boston bank, to enable the construction of a new ballpark in the Hub. He even served as president of the Boston franchise until a suitable buyer stepped forward. Through his efforts the American League debuted in the spring of 1901. In gratitude, Johnson and the other owners elected Somers vice-president of the American

League. He remained a backer of Johnson and a strong voice in league affairs for years to come.

The only standout player in Cleveland's camp at New Orleans was third baseman Bill Bradley. The Cleveland native had jumped the previous season from the Chicago Cubs. "Brad" handled third base as well as anyone in the game, with the possible exception of Boston's Jimmy Collins. Blessed with good power and a cannon for a throwing arm, Bradley stood head and shoulders above his teammates. During the year the New York Giants attempted to steal Bradley away, proposing a three-year guaranteed contract for $10,000. Happy to be home in Cleveland, Bradley turned down the astounding offer. While the locals were pleased Bradley was remaining, they could not have felt quite the same about such marginal players as infielders Frank Bonner and Jack Gochnaur, and catcher Ossee Schreckengost. Despite Bradley's presence, the outfield, featuring the wonderfully named Erwin "Zaza" Harvey, did not exactly create an air of excitement.

Within days of his arrival in camp, Addie showed the players and assembled reporters why Armour had gone to great lengths to acquire him. Displaying a live fastball and sharp curve, he proved to be way ahead of the hitters he faced in practice games. Standing six foot three and weighing 185 pounds, he good naturedly accepted his new nickname: "The Human Slat." Throughout his career, maintaining a healthy weight remained a constant problem. Only twice did his weight reach 200 pounds, and that occurred in the winter months on a steady diet of home cooking. Some considered him frail, but Addie kept himself in good condition. As pitchers were expected to do in those days, he completed most of his starts. He experienced no arm problems until the end of his career. For the most part he took his regular turn and pitched nine innings.

In training camp, Addie became a popular figure with teammates and reporters alike. He was affable and easy-going, and he even got along well with veteran ballplayers who resented college boys and anyone trying to take their jobs away. Articulate and educated, he provided sportswriters with good quotes for their dispatches to Cleveland. Through his whole career, he complimented the players behind him when he won and accepted the blame when he lost, despite a frequent lack of support in the early days. His work ethic and his sportsmanship made him one of the most well-liked players in the American League. He was not the hard drinking, illiterate, brawler that was the stereotype ballplayer of the era. He was the kind of player that Ban Johnson wanted to present to the public to woo ladies and children to American League ballparks.

On rare occasions Addie's long fuse burned to its end, and he exploded in displays of temper. He once flung his glove point blank at the home-plate umpire, earning a five-day suspension that forced him to miss a turn in the rotation. In a game against Philadelphia, Addie fielded a bunt, wheeled, and fired towards first, only to see the ball bouncing down the right field line all the way to the fence. Nobody had covered first, the go-ahead run had scored, and the batter had waltzed all the way to third. While his temper flared, Addie ignored all signs from catcher Harry Bemis, firing fastballs until the side was retired. Between innings he sat alone on the bench, while the remaining Naps positioned themselves as far away from him as possible.

Addie, much like his father Jacob, had a tendency to be generous to a fault. In later years, he invited Theresa down to Cleveland for a visit. While they strolled around the city streets, a panhandler approached them, begging for a handout. Instinctively, Addie reached into his wallet, producing a dollar bill for the man. Theresa shook her head in disbelief, appalled that her son so easily parted with his hard-earned money. Addie simply shrugged.

In mid-April as the Cleveland squad left New Orleans to play their way home in exhibition games planned to help defray spring training costs, Addie got a shocking wire. Charles Strobel had obtained an indictment against him. The charge claimed that Addie had accepted Strobel's $150 advance under false pretenses, a felony punishable by jail time. Addie had returned only $100, and never gave a public explanation for pocketing the remaining $50. The Cleveland owners made good on their pledge to shield Addie from possible problems. Kilfoyl prepared a statement asserting that the charges were without merit. He alleged that Strobel had sent a threatening letter to Theresa Joss, the contents of which justified review by the district attorney's office.

While both sides jockeyed for position, the Cleveland club learned that a sheriff's deputy had received orders to proceed to Columbus, Ohio and arrest Addie when the Bluebirds's train passed through en route to Cleveland. Somers and Kilfoyl acted quickly, spiriting Addie off the train before Columbus. To seize the upper hand, Addie traveled quietly to Toledo, accompanied by a lawyer representing the ballclub. He surrendered to the authorities there, posting bail of $500. A trial date was set for May 1, allowed him to rejoin the team for the inaugural series against St. Louis. Stating to the press that he considered the entire proceedings a farce, Addie shifted his focus to his major league debut, scheduled for Saturday, April 26. He was his new team's fourth starter, behind ex-Dayton star Earl Moore, Luther "Dummy" Taylor, and Gene Wright.

After dropping the first two games, Cleveland scored its first victory of the year, behind Gene Wright's two-hit shutout. Caught up in the excitement, Addie boldly predicted to Henry Edwards of the Cleveland *Plain Dealer*, "If Wright could hold them down to two hits, I will hold 'em to four."

The early days of modern baseball did not provide for much scouting of other teams. The St. Louis batters noted the thick, curly, brown hair spilling out from the cap perched high on top of Addie's head, but they did not have the slightest notion of what to expect from the tall figure peering at them from atop the mound. The first three men went down quickly, fooled by sharp curveballs that darted under their wrists. In the bottom of the second, Addie reached back for some fast ones, striking out the side with just ten pitched balls. The spectators in Sportsman's Park sat quietly along the grandstand, their mouths hanging open in disbelief.

Something had to be done quickly to stop the Cleveland rookie from humiliating the veteran players brought in to represent the American League's newest franchise. When Addie strode to the mound for the bottom of the third inning, he spied old-timers Jack O'Connor and Jesse Burkett taking positions in the coaching boxes. Seeing his cue from O'Connor, Burkett yelled across the diamond, "So you are the guy that came up from Toledo to show us how to play ball are you, Jack?" "Yes I'm it, I broke that Inter-State all to pieces, and thought I'd come up and show you mugs how to pitch," O'Connor shouted back. Burkett answered, "Well, well, you long-legged toothpick, if you don't stop working so hard you'll lose your bonnet!" While the St. Louis fans roared with laughter, O'Connor screamed, "Oh, no, I won't! It's pinned to my curly locks!" In spite of the baiting, Addie stayed calm, chewing fiercely on a wad of gum while keeping the Browns in check. At the end of the fourth inning, Addie shuffled off the mound finding his path blocked by both O'Connor and Burkett. They forced him to detour around them to reach the Cleveland bench. This behavior was standard operating procedure in the baseball of the early 1900s. To counter the verbal abuse and physical intimidation, he had to ignore it and continue to pitch effectively until the loudmouths came to the conclusion their antics were being wasted.

The main instigator, Jesse Burkett, led off the bottom of the sixth inning, lifting a pop fly to short right field. Outfielder Erwin "Zaza" Harvey raced in on the dead run, sliding to his knees to catch the ball off his shoe tops. However Umpire Carruthers did not move from behind home plate, remaining in a poor position to make the call. He ruled that the ball touched the ground, allowing Burkett to remain at first base, and killing Addie's chance to pitch a no-hitter in his first major league start. The Cleveland players rushed Carruthers, arguing that the ball had been caught well off the grass. The argument continued until Carruthers threatened to clear the field, effectively ending the heated discussions.

Cleveland broke the scoreless deadlock in the seventh, tallying three runs. With runners at first and second and one run home, Addie launched a drive to deep right field. The ball landed in the bleachers, smacking a post and rebounding back onto the field. While rounding the bases with the apparent home run, Addie noticed Umpire Carruthers motioning him back to second base. The umpire had decided the hit was a ground-rule double, although he allowed the run to score from first base. Another altercation ensued, yielding similar results as the first.

Hundreds of miles away in Cleveland, interest in the Bluebirds had risen to such a level that the *Plain Dealer* had decided to provide a play-by-play telegraph service for rabid fans. The crowd gathered in front of the newspaper building grew throughout this game. Addie did not disappoint, holding the Browns to one disputed hit in winning his first game, 3-0. Cleveland fans buzzed with excitement, hoping that Addie truly represented the real thing.

Relaxing at dinner that evening, Addie smiled when waiters brought a large arrangement of carnations to the table. The head waiter handed one to Addie, who pinned it to his lapel. He ate dinner at a leisurely pace, and headed up to his room to collapse for the night. Climbing the stairs, he was startled to see St. Louis outfielder Emmit Heidrich waiting on the landing. Braced for the worst, Addie stopped in his tracks. Years later he recounted Heidrich's words. Showing off his worst scowl, the outfielder snarled "Think so well of yourself you wear flowers, do you? Wait until we get at you again, you human sign post, and what we'll do to you will make you long for the bushes!" Addie waited uncertainly, ready for Heidrich to make a rush at him. Suddenly Heidrich smiled and extended his right arm, saying, "Shake hands kid, you pitched a great game!" The day certainly belonged to Addie who stopped the Browns from taking the series. He came within a judgment call of recording a no-hitter in his very first American League game. People slowly started to take notice of the "Human Slat."

After a loss to Chicago in which he allowed five walks, Addie returned to Toledo to appear before the grand jury. The Cleveland attorney moved that the case be dismissed. The grand jury deliberated for several minutes, then did as Addie's lawyer had asked, citing a lack of evidence. To make sure that the case would go away for good, Somers and Kilfoyl gave Strobel and the Mud Hens a prospect. Several years later, when the smoke had cleared, Addie bought a home in Toledo, settling down with his wife as a full time resident. He renewed friendships, remaining in Toledo for the rest of his life. He even tried to buy the Mud Hens, but the price tag remained a bit too high for him and his partner, Giants catcher Roger Bresnahan.

Able to concentrate on baseball exclusively, Addie rejoined the Bluebirds for their series in Detroit. Having lost three straight, Cleveland hoped to salvage the final game and avoid the embarrassment of a sweep. Since the concluding contest fell on a Sunday, the Detroit management held the game on the outskirts of the city to avoid the condemnation of the clergy. When the Tigers took the field for the start of the game, no fewer than 7,000 spectators poured into the tiny wooden bleachers of West End Park. Part of the overflow crowd stood on the playing field. Addie repeated his St. Louis feat, this time holding Detroit hitless for eight innings. As Cleveland prepared for the final inning, things got downright ugly. Fans climbed out of the stands, forming a semicircle around the infield. Frustrated Tiger rooters lined up at third base, forming a line down to home plate and around to first base. They shoved their way to within twenty feet of the playing field, setting off an alarm among the Cleveland players. Bill Armour pleaded with the handful of police to do something, but the cops simply shrugged, unwilling to start a riot. Armour then demanded the umpire to forfeit the game to Cleveland, but his request was denied.

Addie tried to ignore the epithets hurled at him, retiring the first batter in the ninth. With Ducky Holmes at bat, the insults rose another notch, determined to break Addie's concentration. Holmes, taking advantage of the crowd's interference, bunted down the third base line. Bill Bradley came charging in but fumbled the ball while Holmes raced safely to first. A single by Doc Casey ruined Addie's second serious bid for a no-hitter in three starts, but he hung on, retiring the final batter on a bouncer back to the box. Cleveland won the game, 2-1. Addie kept his composure, and his calmness during the wild final inning won him the praise of the Detroit newspapers. The *News* wrote, "Joss is a great pitcher, and on form displayed in a game on the links of West End Park, it must be said that he is the peer of anybody who has yet limbered up in this country. Inning after inning the Detroit batters didn't bat, not a hit coming in the first eight, and only four men reaching first."

In twenty-seven innings of pitching, Addie had allowed only five runs, two of them unearned. He exhibited poise and concentration of a pitcher many years older. He had established himself as the ace of the Cleveland staff.

With the extended road trip concluded, the Bluebirds assembled at League Park to prepare for their home opener the following day. The afternoon workout drew a crowd of more than 1,000. Certainly the fans had great expectations for a team that had given no evidence of being a pennant contender. But this was part of the spirit of the city in those days. Clevelanders thought of their town as progressive and modern. Downtown made the transition from large shade trees to skyscrapers. In his book *Cleveland: The Making of a City*, William Rose described the progress. "Some people objected to the change and there was an increasing number who moved to the suburbs to escape the hustle bustle of the rapidly growing industrial and commercial center. Many fled to avoid the noise and smoke served up by the automobiles which crowded the highways."

A survey indicated a total of 476 autos were registered at an average cost of $1,500. At the turn of the century Cleveland rivaled Detroit as a manufacturer of passenger cars. Companies such as Winton Motor Carriage Company and Baker Electric produced quality autos that sold at a healthy pace. Shipbuilding and the railroad industry thrived locally, contributing to

Addie at the beginning of his career with Cleveland.

Cleveland's status as an important commerce center of the Midwest. Wealthy industrialists gravitated to the city, the most noteworthy being John D. Rockefeller, who built a fashionable country estate equipped with a private golf course. Important national politicians abounded, among them Senator Marcus Hanna and Secretary of State John Hay. It seemed the only entity not challenging for supremacy was the Cleveland Bluebirds.

Opening day ceremonies produced much color and excitement to those who braved the cold of an early spring Ohio afternoon. Addie rode with fellow teammates on special carriages provided for both teams. They were flanked by no fewer than three marching bands hired to provide spirited tunes to entertain the spectators lining Ontario and Superior Avenues. The parade wound its way through downtown streets, eventually marching down Euclid Avenue east to League Park. Spurred on by the ardent loyalty of its fans, Cleveland promptly blew the opener, losing to St. Louis, 6-4.

On May 12, 1902, a crowd of 3,000 witnessed Addie's initial appearance in a home uniform. They observed a sub par performance, which resulted in a 7-2 loss. Addie failed to get the ball over the plate, walking eleven batters and hitting two more. Starts like these reminded Bill Armour that Addie still needed experience in the league to become a reliable workhorse.

In spite of the occasional fits of wildness, he still represented the best pitcher Cleveland had to offer, as he waited for reinforcements to shore up the shoddy play of his teammates. Outside of Bill Bradley, the best defensive player on the Bluebirds was located on the mound. Addie fielded his position remarkably well, using his height to snare bounders up the middle, while handling bunts as skillfully as any pitcher in the game. He recorded a lot of assists during his career, and committed few errors. The Philadelphia *North American* joked about his long arms and defensive prowess. "With Joss on the slab it looks like bad judgment for Cleveland to employ infielders. His right hand reached almost to third base and his left was capable of scooping up balls along the first base line."

Wholesale changes in Cleveland's lineup found Addie filling in at first base between turns on the mound. As Charles Somers searched for a regular at the position, Addie manned the bag as he had done at Juneau High School. Unfortunately, Addie hit like a pitcher, flailing away at the ball while his teammates winced at the sight. He returned to the mound against St. Louis, but four costly errors behind him resulted in a 5-0 loss. In an eleven-inning loss to Boston, errors and careless base running cost Cleveland the game. Reminded of the plays which led to defeat, Addie responded to the *Plain Dealer*'s query, "It was my fault and no one else's. But for me they would not have had a run. In the fifth inning with two strikes on Cy Young the ball slipped out of my hand and Cy hit it out for a single, allowing Boston to tie the score. Had that ball not have slipped we would have won."

Charles Somers saw that he had to make some moves. He knew that Connie Mack had legal problems with his cross-town rivals over ex-Phillies Napoleon Lajoie, Elmer Flick, and Bill Bernhard. The previous year Mack had scored a major victory by persuading the trio to jump to his Athletics. Furious at their defection, Phillies owner Colonel John Rogers successfully obtained injunctions against Lajoie and Bernhard, barring them from playing ball in Pennsylvania — which meant that they could not appear at home. Seeing that Flick might suffer the same fate, Somers, to whom Mack owed so much, persuaded the Athletics's leader to relinquish his rights to the outfielder so that Cleveland could sign him and keep him in the American League. He also got permission to negotiate with Lajoie and Bernhard. Within weeks all three players wore Bluebird uniforms, transforming the team from pretenders to contenders. During 1902, Somers had to keep two of his new players out of Pennsylvania when Cleveland faced the Athletics, but the following year the peace treaty between the two leagues freed Lajoie and Bernhard to compete in the city of brotherly love.

To complete the restructuring of personnel, Somers signed fleet outfielder Harry Bay to a contract. Nicknamed "Sliver" for his lack of size, and "Deerfoot" for his speed, Bay patrolled center field, while Flick covered the territory in right. Cleveland's defense, particularly up the middle, improved dramatically. The team appointed Larry Lajoie, along with Honus Wagner one of baseball's two best players, captain, and declared the team would now be known simply as the Blues.

With a full complement of players, Addie's confidence grew. At the end of May he beat the Washington Senators, 7-2. At one point in the game, he unleashed a fastball so potent that catcher Harry Bemis could not hold on to it. Each pitch bounced off the catcher's glove, ping-ponging halfway up the pitchers mound. Tough as nails, the 150-pound Bemis hung in there, gamely trying to control the rockets fired at him. For all his great speed, Addie preferred to use all his pitches to keep hitters off balance, and he never tried to strike everyone out. When he had his best stuff, the game summary usually showed the first baseman with many putouts and the outfielders with few. Batter after batter pounded the ball into the ground, where the sure-handed Bradley or Lajoie made the play.

At the 1902 season's midpoint, Addie turned in several remarkable performances. He beat Detroit 3-0, allowing only two doubles. Nine days later he duplicated the feat, holding the Tigers to three hits in a 2-0 win. Addie retired the last thirteen men he faced, completing the game in less than ninety minutes. He continued to pitch exceptionally into August, when he faced Boston and the great veteran Cy Young. Through five innings Addie clung to a 2-0 lead. In the bottom of the fifth he led off with a single, ready to take second on the expected sacrifice by Harry Bay. Young delivered home, where catcher Lou Criger grabbed the ball and faked a throw to first. Addie dove back to the bag, catching his spikes in the turf. He tried to straighten up but felt a sharp pain in his left knee. He had to be helped off the field, unable to put any weight on the rapidly swelling joint. Teams in those days did not employ team doctors or even skilled trainers. Injured players fended for themselves. Addie simply rested in his rooming house until the swelling came down. He was out for seventeen days, forcing Armour to sign sandlot pitchers to fill in until he returned.

Addie limped back to League Park, winning his last two starts to register seventeen wins for the season against thirteen losses. He posted an earned run average of 2.77, while recording five shutouts, best among American League pitchers. He impressed enough ballplayers to be invited to join the All-Americans, a barnstorming team consisting of the top stars who were willing to tour the western states for several months. Win Mercer, Detroit's popular pitcher organized the tour, which called for the team to travel to California, stopping in cities along the way. They were accompanied by the All-Nationals, a similar squad of stars from the senior circuit. Mercer got commitments from Philadelphia's Harry Davis, Topsy Hartsel, and Monte Cross. Chicago's Fielder Jones and Billy Sullivan agreed to accompany the team. From Cleveland, Lajoie, Bradley, Bernhard, and Joss joined the team, though the first two backed out after several games, Lajoie to open a cigar store and Bradley to take it easy. Mercer picked up Bobby Wallace and Dick Padden to replace the dropouts.

The two squads met in Chicago on Thursday, October 12. The All-Nationals unveiled black uniforms, trimmed with gold and yellow lettering. The team consisted of stalwarts like Sam Crawford, Wee Willie Keeler, Jake Beckley, and pitchers Jesse Tannehill and Jack Chesbro. The All-Americans dazzled the crowd with their patriotic uniforms of red, white and blue. Ablaze with stars and stripes, their caps were a brilliant replica of Old Glory.

After a lopsided victory by the All-Nationals, the teams boarded a train bound for Cedar Rapids, Iowa. The schedule called for the teams to play every day until a two-day break in Los Angeles. Fans in Des Moines, Omaha, Topeka, Denver, Albuquerque, El Paso, Tucson, and Phoenix got a chance to see major league baseball performed by the game's top stars. The players took it easy in the early games, conserving their energy for the long haul. A string of victories by the All-Nationals, though, reignited the competitive fires. Addie later wrote of the experience. "It was understood that the trip was for pleasure and while we were to play as good as we knew how, yet it was not a matter of life or death which team won. Up to the time we reached Missouri, the Nationals had put it on us with persistent regularity and were beginning to kid us about our inferior team. This made us feel we were being made sport of and it was but a few days before both teams were sliding into each other with spikes up and fighting tooth and nail for every game." This letter was printed in the Cleveland papers. This item endeared Addie to Cleveland rooters who greatly admired ballplayers of the competitive spirit.

Addie pitched outstanding baseball throughout the trip. He began a win streak that lasted until December 12. On November 20 he pitched eleven innings of shutout ball, beating the All-Nationals, 1-0. He led off the bottom of the eleventh with a double, scoring the game winner on a single. The Los Angeles *Times* wrote, "If this is Joss' first season out he will be a bad one to beat next year."

The teams split up, playing exhibitions against minor league clubs up and down California. In a game against Sacramento, the players went to sleep, allowing the hosts to secure a 2-1 win. Angry with the half-hearted effort, Addie wrote to Bill Armour in Cleveland. "We were simply outplayed and beaten in good shape too. It serves us right and will probably be the best thing that could happen to all of us. The idea that we can go against any team that we meet and beat them offhand is a mistaken one, and this lesson that we have had will set the boys to thinking." The next time out, the All-Americans swept a doubleheader from Oakland, Bill Bernhard pitching a no-hitter in game one.

At year's end the touring squads hooked up again in San Francisco for a three-game series. The American boys swept all three contests in convincing fashion. Addie won the second game, beating Wild Bill Donovan 2-1. The players rested a few days, debating the merits of booking passage to Hawaii for a few games. Finances wouldn't allow this plan to be carried out, and the players decided to stay in San Francisco for a short time, then start the long trek back to Chicago.

Days before their departure a bizarre incident at the players' hotel led to tragedy. With most of the players working out at a local ballpark, a man identifying himself as a messenger for Win

Mercer gave a note to the front desk clerk. The note asked for the large envelope in the hotel safe to be handed over to the messenger for delivery to the field. Without asking for any identification, the clerk retrieved the envelope and handed it to the messenger. A few moments later the man reappeared, saying he'd been given the wrong envelope—the one with rail tickets and schedules. He explained he needed the envelope containing the team receipts. He also asked the clerk for Addie's envelope. Team receipts totaled over $15,000, and Addie's share came to over $600.

This clerk finally become suspicious, and excused himself for a few moments. He found Jack Chesbro, who had stayed back at the hotel, and asked him to dash down to the park and ask if Mercer and Joss knew anything about the messenger. Chesbro quickly returned, with the news that the messenger was a phony. The man bolted from the lobby, racing through the front entrance and out of sight.

Before the dust settled, Win Mercer quietly checked out of the Langham, registering at the Occidental Hotel, a few blocks away. He gave his name as George Murray of Philadelphia. Later that evening, the hotel's watchman smelled gas coming from Mercer's room. He broke down the door, and discovered the gruesome sight of Win Mercer lying dead on the bed. A rubber tube connected to the gas jet in the center of the room dangled from the ceiling next to Mercer's body. He had left several notes, but the only possible clues to his motivation were in a note to a friend, cautioning him to stay away from women and games of chance. Speculation ran rampant that the suicide was connected to the robbery attempt. Rumors persisted that Mercer had lost money to gamblers. Other rumors claimed he suffered from heart disease, which caused him to become despondent.

The death of Mercer finished the tour. Addie volunteered to accompany Mercer's body back to East Liverpool, Ohio, where relatives waited to make funeral arrangements. He spoke nothing of the death to reporters. Whatever he might have known about the tragedy went untold.

Passing through Chicago on his way to Portage, Wisconsin, Addie told reporters he felt in fine shape for the 1903 season. "I pitched as good ball this winter as I ever did," he explained. "Look out for the Cleveland boys when we get started. We are going to be in it from the drop of the hat." Addie had become a recognizable figure from Boston to California. In one season he had moved from untested newcomer to one of the leading pitchers in the game. In Cleveland, he entered the 1903 season second only to the great Lajoie in popularity.

Stardom

ANXIOUS TO RELAX FOR THE NEXT SEVERAL MONTHS, Addie arrived in Portage to visit with Theresa. He brought with him the newest addition to the Joss family, his bride, Lillian Shinavar. On the eve of the All-American tour, Addie had detoured to Monroe, Michigan where Lillian waited to become Mrs. Joss. Just across the Ohio border, Monroe provided a service for Ohioans who were aware of the no waiting period for marriage licenses in the Wolverine state. On Saturday evening, October 11, 1902, Addie and Lillian had been married in the living room of Judge Matthews. After one night with his bride, Addie had departed for Chicago and the cross country tour.

Addie had chosen for his bride a dark-haired, dark-eyed Toledo beauty almost three years his senior. They had been an item for several years, after being introduced by a mutual friend after a Mud Hens game. Lillian had grown up in northwest Ohio, the daughter of Michael and Mary Shinavar. Michael earned a living the hard way, taking jobs wherever he could find them. At various times he worked as a laborer, a groom, a coachman, and a hack driver. Although the family had little money, Lillian got a good enough education to find work as a court stenographer. On occasional trips to the ballpark she fell hard for the Elongated Twirler.

Addie's hasty decision to join the All-Americans probably spoiled plans for a festive fall wedding. Lillian quickly got a taste of what life with a ballplayer would be like. Upon his return, Addie brought Lillian to meet the folks in and around Portage, then left her again to accompany the Juneau town bowling team to Milwaukee. Weeks later he packed his grip for spring training, and dropped Lillian off in Toledo. This was all par for the course. Ballplayers generally left their wives and children at home. Players lived in hotels and boarding houses during the season, often doubling up with a teammate. They lived together, ate together, practiced together, and spent virtually all their time as a unit. When the season closed, many of them took to the road barnstorming or joined the ever popular vaudeville circuit.

Addie gradually changed his ways over the years. The addition of two children made him much more of a homebody. He bought his first and only home on Fulton Street in Toledo, establishing a base only a short train ride from Cleveland. When the Blues passed through town on western trips, Addie always asked for a day off to see his family. At the close of training camp, he caught the first train north, rushing home to spend a couple of days with Lillian and the children. Lillian often had snapshots taken of son Norman and daughter Ruth, sending them to Addie down south. The kids eagerly awaited their father's return, knowing there would be a suitcase full of toys to play with. In 1909, Addie broke tradition, bringing the entire family to Mobile, Alabama for spring training. After workouts he positioned Norman on the field, teaching him the early basics of the game. When photographers lined up the players for the team picture, Addie placed his small son in the front row. During the off-season, Addie made up for lost time, spending most of the winter at home. He bought sleds for the children, dragging them through the abundant snowfalls of the colder months. Christmas became a major event in the Joss home, with singing and dancing around the lavishly decorated tree. Addie cherished his new name of "Papa," devoting countless hours to his family. While he was away he sent a steady stream of letters back home, reminding Norman he was temporarily the man of the family, and to always look after his younger sister. After the children arrived, Addie was always homesick on the road.

The Blues returned to New Orleans for spring training, 1903. Great things were expected of the team, which had played quality ball since Lajoie and company had come aboard. Everyone was optimistic. Even the mandatory three-mile walk to the local gymnasium for daily workouts went without complaint. (In the gym, the players tried to convince Flick and Bemis, both with reputations as fighters, to put on the boxing gloves. They refused, but Bemis showed his ability several years later in a brawl with Ty Cobb at home plate. A bone-jarring collision between the two resulted in the tiny catcher dropping the ball. Furious at Cobb's rough play, Bemis scrambled to his feet, charged the much bigger Cobb and landed several shots before both teams entered the fray.)

Upon completion of the afternoon's practice, the players shuffled off to the St. Charles Hotel to clean up for dinner. Once the food had been plundered, most gathered in the lobby to relax and swap stories. This year, Addie had good material of his own to match the exaggerations of his teammates. He related an incident that had taken place on the All-American tour. "I played my first game in the outfield at Omaha," he told curious listeners. "The score was 4-4 and the Nationals had a man on third when Keeler came to bat in the ninth inning. He knocked a high fly back of second and I came in like Harry Bay, only that I came in faster. Well, I caught the ball and it was a beautiful catch if I do say it myself. In fact I was thinking about what a great outfielder I was and forgot all about the man on third base. When I woke up the run had crossed the plate and we were beaten 5-4."

Addie, still a few weeks shy of his twenty-third birthday, assumed the role of veteran ballplayer. With all the personnel changes made on the roster, he had rapidly acquired seniority. Only Bill Bradley and Earl Moore had longer service. As one of the elders he happily took his place in the "fanning bees," displaying a dry sense of humor that drew an audience of players and rooters alike. He enjoyed stretching out his long frame on one of the easy chairs, sitting for hours and participating in the evening discussions. In Cleveland he frequented Lajoie's cigar shop, crowding into the small store with teammates, visiting players, and rabid Cleveland fans. One evening Clark Griffith and several of his New York players stopped to visit. Griffith began to ride Addie, telling him he was all washed up, and the rest of the League knew it. After several minutes of harassment, Addie stood up and faced his tormentors, predicting they would eat their words the next day. True to his warning, Addie threw a three hit shutout to throttle the Highlanders, 3-0.

When not engaged in storytelling, the players took to singing to pass the long hours between practices. Addie had a good voice which he often exhibited to small crowds in hotel lobbies on the road, and he joined a barbershop quartet, which practiced nightly at the St. Charles. Harry Bay, who with his wife had toured the vaudeville circuit the previous winter, served as unofficial manager of the group. He tried to recruit the quartet for his musical act, but the boys declined when they learned that the occasional rotten tomato might be tossed from the audience. Addie eventually gave in to the temptation and appeared on the vaudeville circuit around Chicago.

Spending a great deal of time together, the players developed a strong sense of camaraderie, often characterized by jokes and insults. Addie was an easy target for barbs about his lack of bulk and his rural background. Depending on the day, he could expect to be called Slat, Stick, Signpost, and Hairpin. When teammates, particularly Bill Bradley, got zeroed in, they asked innocent questions about the size of Juneau and the residents there. City boy Bradley enjoyed needling Addie about his hometown. He encouraged Addie to run for mayor because he'd only need four or five votes to carry the election. Addie's Swiss-German descent also came under scrutiny. One sportswriter peppered him with questions until he had finally had enough. Addie calmly informed the curious writer that he was, in fact, a direct descendant of William Tell, and would gladly prove it to the writer by knocking a baseball off his head at sixty feet. The reporter politely declined the invitation.

Other players came in for their share of kidding. Bill Bernhard was called "Sara" for the popular actress of the stage, Charlie Hickman became "Piano Legs" for obvious reasons, and lithe Harry Bay answered to "Sliver."

The team broke camp stopping in Indianapolis for a tune-up before the season's opener. Addie pitched five strong innings, fanning eight batters while not allowing a base on balls. He pitched the opener, losing, 4-2, to Detroit in weather conditions reminiscent of early November. The Blues lost all three games and limped home to Cleveland to kick off the home schedule. The defeats failed to dampen the unbridled enthusiasm of the baseball crazies in town. Demand for tickets was such that Charley Somers hired a work crew to build temporary bleachers in right field. On opening day thousands lined up outside League Park, attempting to buy tickets that sold out within an hour. Attendance was 19,867, the largest crowd ever to see professional baseball in Cleveland. Fans perched themselves on rooftops and outfield fences, while thousands stood behind ropes on the playing field. Young boys who couldn't see over the adults standing in front of them scrambled to find empty coke bottles. They turned the bottles neck first, jamming the open ends in the ground where they stood. Using an adult for balance, they hopped on the bottles, one under each foot, holding on to the man directly in front.

Addie jogged to the mound wearing the spotless new flannels issued that morning. The shirts and pants were white, with socks and belts contrasting in deep maroon. The caps were white, with a maroon C above the bill. The players were given white sweaters to wear when traveling to and from the park. For the road, the traditional navy blue uniforms were retained, offset by a new design of blue and white socks.

Addie got off to a rocky start, walking the St. Louis leadoff hitter, Jesse Burkett. A single to center brought Burkett home with the game's first run. The Blues answered in the bottom of the second inning when Addie drove the ball to right field, scoring the tying run. After Harry Bay flied out, a double by Jack McCarthy scored Addie and Harry Bemis with the lead runs. Cleveland scored single runs in the third and fourth to go ahead, 5-1. While Addie protected the lead, the temporary bleachers began to shudder, provoking the fans to panic and jump out to the field. Seconds later the hastily constructed wooden stands collapsed, leaving a tumbling mass of arms and legs flailing about the outfield grounds. Two men were trampled on, both taken away unconscious by horse drawn ambulances. Amazingly there were few other injuries, and the game continued after the dazed spectators got back on their feet. Addie allowed two more runs, but the Blues won the home opener, 6-3. After the game he took a train to Toledo to escort Lillian to Theresa Joss' two-family home in Portage for the summer.

After losing seven of their first nine games, the Blues needed some luck to snap them out of their lethargic play. In a home contest against the Detroit Tigers, the game was tied going in to the late innings. Addie entered the game at first base, due to some lineup-shuffling required when Bill Bradley was tossed for arguing with the umpire. Leading off the bottom of the eighth, Addie drilled a single. The spring weather was still cool, and the janitor of the apartment building behind the left field fence chose this moment to fire up the furnace. He used too much coal in the process, and created a huge cloud of smoke which drifted over left field. Before the Tigers could call time, shortstop Jack Gochnaur lifted a towering fly ball to left. Sam Crawford lost sight of it in the smoke, and Addie scored with the winning run. Though some felt the janitor was paid off by Cleveland management for his part in the victory, the win stood, helping the Blues get back on track.

Hazards on the playing field were a fairly common phenomenon of the dead ball days. The most prominent obstacle came in the form of overflow crowds. Owners had no qualms about placing excess fans on the field, cutting the size of the playing area in the process. Batted balls that fell in to the mass of humanity were counted as doubles. As the collapsed grandstand in Cleveland illustrates, safety was not a high priority to baseball magnates. A similar incident occurred in Detroit several years later during a doubleheader with the Blues. Fortunately, few spectators suffered serious injuries that time, either.

The following season, Cleveland played at Philadelphia, where an overflow crowd of 18,000 packed the stadium. Elmer Flick fearlessly chased a pop fly drifting toward the overflow crowd behind the right field line. At the last instant Flick reached out his glove, diving head first in to the wall of people along the line. He did not make the catch, but he collided with the sandwich vendor, spraying mustard and ham all over the crowd. Other obstacles frequently came into play, too. At home against Boston, Addie was dueling Cy Young in a tight game. With a runner on base, Young lifted a fly ball into the right field corner. It dropped right into a hole under the grandstand. While Flick tried to burrow under the stands, Young rumbled around the bases, tallying the winning run. Such was life in the years long before the existence of professional grounds crews.

Coinciding with the Blues' improving play, Addie launched an impressive string of pitching performances. Traveling to Philadelphia, the squad included Lajoie and Bernhard, who were finally free to return to the city uninhibited by legal constraints. The game against the Athletics pitted the two old adversaries from Wisconsin semipro days, Waddell and Joss. Neither had forgotten their match up in Racine two years before, and both pitchers pulled out all the stops. Addie retired the first fifteen batters he faced, while Waddell blew hitters out of the batter's box with fastballs that all but left a trail of smoke. In the top of the sixth inning, Bill Bradley singled to drive in Harry Bay with the game's initial run. Addie got himself in trouble in the bottom half, throwing an inside fastball that struck shortstop Monte Cross on the right calf. A sacrifice moved Cross to second, bringing Waddell up to bat. Addie wasted little time with his adversary, sending him back to the bench on strikes. With two outs, lead off hitter Topsy Hartsel lined a single past Bill Bradley to tie the game at one.

Both pitchers bore down, neither allowing another run. Addie had perfect control, keeping the ball away from the Athletic hitters, while Waddell continued to pile up the strikeouts. In the top of the eleventh he showed awesome power, using only ten pitches to fan in succession Harry Bay, Larry Lajoie, and Bill Bradley. In the top of the fourteenth, the Blues got runners at first and second with only one out. Flick stepped to the plate, only to become Waddell's fourteenth strikeout victim. Charlie Hickman tried to steal third, but failed to beat the tag, ending the inning. The umpire informed both benches that the bottom of the inning would be the last, due to darkness. Addie retired the first batter, bringing former Blues outfielder Ollie Pickering to the plate. He took two strikes, then lifted Addie's third offering deep into the right field screen to win the game, 2-1. While fans dashed on the field to mob Pickering, Addie stood motionless on the mound. The *Plain Dealer* likened Addie's posture to a "sunflower going to sleep at the close of the day." Though deeply disappointed by the outcome, he had pitched a tremendous game. His statistics showed thirteen and a third innings pitched, six hits, two runs, eight strikeouts and no bases on balls. Facing forty-seven batters and not allowing a walk illustrates how precise Addie's control had become. He was now a complete pitcher, one of the best in the game.

Buoyed by Addie's fine pitching, the Blues won thirteen out of fourteen games in August, inching their way toward second place. On August 22 Philadelphia returned to League Park for another duel between Joss and Waddell. At game time, Rube executed one of his infamous vanishing acts, leaving Connie Mack mystified. A search of the neighborhood saloons failed to turn up the elusive star, forcing Mack to use Eddie Plank, no slouch, a day early. Blues fans hoping for a spectacular rematch were disappointed.

Addie allowed a hit in the sixth inning, and recorded the second one-hitter of his career. In the top of the second he needed just three pitches to retire the side. The 3-0 win marked Addie's eighteenth victory of the season. With over a month remaining, he seemed a sure bet to win twenty. Six days later the Blues left Cleveland for St. Louis. The players stopped in Toledo to join the Browns on a special train, carrying only two sleeper cars for the players and a single baggage car to haul the luggage and game equipment. Addie shared a compartment with Charlie Hickman, who took the top berth. As the train chugged out of northwest Ohio most of the players were sleeping soundly, but Earl Moore had a premonition of disaster. He peered out the window while the train approached the crossing of the Wabash and Detroit Southern tracks. Traveling at forty miles an hour, the train entered the crossing, where the derailer had not been properly set. The engineer frantically slammed on the emergency brake, but the train jumped the track and crashed, landing sideways in a large ditch. The dazed players found themselves in total darkness, smoke filling the air around them. At the moment of impact, Hickman flew out of his berth, landing on top of Addie. The force of the crash and the weight of "Piano Legs" rendered Addie unconscious. He recovered quickly, having the presence of mind to reach up and smash the window at the top of the car. Bobby Wallace, the St. Louis shortstop, heard the window break and scrambled over to pull Addie and Hickman out of the car. Within minutes all the players were accounted for, miraculously escaping serious injury. The baggage car lay nearby, smashed so severely that the players' possessions went unrecovered.

Despite the near disaster, the Blues made light of the crash, cracking jokes about the experience. Addie told the Cleveland *Press*, "I thought it was the engine on top of me but it was only Hick. When Hick falls on you from a distance of five or six feet you know it all right" Shaken, the teams boarded another train for St. Louis. Addie eventually collected a check for $300, to cover his lost baggage and his "inconvenience." The next day, the two teams played their afternoon game as if nothing unusual had happened the previous evening. Addie won his nineteenth game, 7-4, going the distance.

The Blues departed St. Louis for a series in Detroit. On the ride through Michigan Addie was floored by a fever that soared over 100 degrees. He also had a headache and a cough. Alarmed at the sudden attack, Bill Armour put Addie on a train for home and telegraphed to Cleveland to coordinate arrangements for an ambulance to pick Addie up at Union Station and rush him to the hospital. At the hospital, doctors at first feared typhoid fever, but

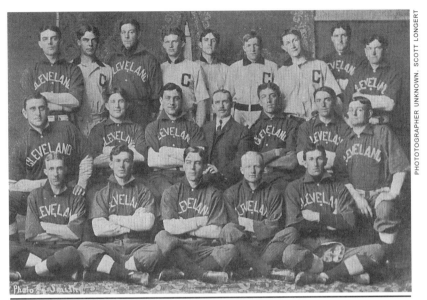

The 1904 Cleveland Blues. TOP ROW (L TO R): *Moore, Rossman, Donohue, Hess, Curtiss, Pastor, Schwartz, Hickey, Rhoades.* SECOND ROW: *Bernhard, Abbott, Lajoie, Armour, Joss, Hickman, Flick.* BOTTOM ROW: *Bay, Bemis, O'Hara, Turner, Bradley.*

quickly ruled it out because none of the other players had become ill. Addie remained in the hospital while doctors tried to bring his temperature down. It was two weeks before the fever finally broke. Addie was so weakened that he had to walk with a cane. He lost weight, and was out for the entire month of September. No cause was ever discovered. It may be that he suffered undetected internal injuries in the train wreck.

With the fever went Addie's chance to win twenty or even twenty-five games in his six or seven remaining starts. Despite the setback, he boasted a fine record of nineteen wins, thirteen losses and four shutouts. Lajoie captured the batting title, Harry Bay led the American League in stolen bases, Bill Bradley finished second in triples, and first baseman Charlie Hickman blasted twelve home runs. Boston won the pennant, Cleveland had looked good enough to inspire optimism for the next campaign.

Addie stayed in Cleveland until he felt strong enough to travel to Portage. In October he left town, anxious to get back to his family. He spent the winter relaxing, playing cards with Lillian and Theresa. He put in overtime at the dinner table, gaining back the weight he had lost and then some.

After the unsuccessful attempt to buy the Mud Hens from Charles Strobel, Addie began preparations for another trip to spring training. Somers selected San Antonio, Texas as the 1904 practice site. Somers believed the hot, humid conditions would benefit the out-of-shape, overweight ballplayers. After a grueling twenty-hour train ride, the Blues assembled for their initial workouts. All of them marveled at the weather conditions, which dropped the pounds off quickly. The blazing sun warmed up the pitchers arms so they could throw with no strain on their elbows. Addie worked hard the first week, wearing himself out in the humid air. He took part in daily infield practice, filling in for Bradley and Hickman whenever possible. He rarely took a break, either throwing to Harry Bemis or fielding ground balls with the regulars. He delighted in giving pitching instructions to the new recruits brought west by Bill Armour. He did not see young pitchers as a threat, handling them as he would a veteran. Before long, local pitchers gravitated to the Blues camp, where Addie made the time to conduct informal clinics on the fine points of the art.

The therapeutic effects of training in San Antonio quickly dissipated. Addie and several other pitchers developed sore arms from overextending themselves. To keep active, Addie played second base in the intra-squad games, drawing rave reviews from the San Antonio fans. His infield skills were good enough for Bill Armour to use him in emergencies during regular season play. His performance at the plate kept him from being a competent utility ballplayer. Addie's hitting was horrendous. He often struck out two or three times a game. With his unusually large strike zone, pitchers had a field day against him. In his entire career he managed only one home run, that in a losing cause to Detroit.

After practice the Blues scurried back to the St. George Hotel to escape the blistering heat. Gradually most of the players assembled in the lobby for the evening's fanning bee. One topic of conversation was the fact that players were easy targets for con men anxious to fleece them out of their savings. The players referred to the crooks as "promoters," who tried to sell them stocks or investment deals which inevitably went sour. Lajoie, Armour, Moore, and Pirates third baseman Tommy Leach all bought stock together in an oil company at fifty dollars a share. Within a month the stock plummeted to twelve, leaving the group with a huge loss. Bill Bradley invested five hundred dollars in an automobile company only to see the funds and the company vanish. Lajoie remarked philosophically, "I guess all ballplayers are easy. These promoters who are looking for easy marks camp on our trail until they land us." The average ballplayer was unsophisticated and easily bilked. An astute promoter recognized a player as someone with ready cash and not much education in how to handle it properly. After a convincing sales pitch, the unsuspecting mark often found himself giving away chunks of money which invariably disappeared along with the promoter. There is no record that Addie ever fell victim to any schemes. The near loss of his earnings from the All-American tour may well have caused him to be extra-cautious with his savings.

At the end of one evening, Addie related his version of the perfect game for a pitcher. "It is after he has pitched and won, say an eleven inning game, holding the opposing team down to four or five hits. Then he goes to the clubhouse and has a nice bath, goes to supper and then to sleep on his performance and gets up in the morning and reads what the papers have to say about him." When asked what he does when he gets batted around all over the field, Addie replied with a straight face, "Well, that morning I don't read the papers."

Early in the season, Addie awoke in his rooming house on Belvedere Street again wracked with cough and fever. Once again he made a trip to the hospital. The doctors were again concerned with the possibility of typhoid fever, because the new Blues shortstop, Terry Turner, had come down with the typhoid several days earlier. The prevailing opinion blamed unsanitary conditions at the San Antonio site. Fortunately Addie did not contract typhoid, but the fever lingered long enough for him to miss five weeks of the season. He attempted to pitch against Washington on June 18, but had to retire after three innings. He rested another ten days before pitching again, this time going the distance in a 4-0 shutout of St. Louis. He scattered three hits while not walking a man in a fast-paced game, completed in just sixty nine minutes. Despite the strong outing, Addie felt completely exhausted after the game. He appeared sporadically for the next month, sitting out six or seven days between starts. Not until the end of July did he feel strong enough to join the regular rotation. Addie defeated Cy Young at Boston, throwing a six-hit shutout. Cleveland celebrated Addie's return by touching up Cy for seventeen hits in its 9-0 victory.

In mid August Addie hit his stride, beating Washington, 1-0, in a game that went twelve innings. The Blues lone run came on a single by first baseman George Stovall and a double by Terry Turner. In the bottom of the twelfth the Senators threatened, placing runners on first and third with two out. Addie calmly struck out the final hitter to chalk up his eleventh strikeout of the game. He allowed only four hits in his best showing of the season.

Though Cleveland languished out of contention, Addie pitched remarkable ball, allowing no more than one run in six straight appearances. With virtually no hitting behind him, he lost three times by the score of 1-0. He completed the season with fourteen wins, nine defeats, and the best earned run average in both leagues: 1.59. He had five shutouts, while walking only thirty batters in 192 innings. In spite of the early season illness, he posted excellent numbers for the year.

On September 7 Bill Armour announced his resignation. Frustrated by his team's inability to win the pennant, Armour decided he could no longer continue on the job. Cleveland had three future Hall of Famers—Flick, Joss, and Lajoie—and fine players like Bay and Bradley, all in their primes. Armour has been accused of putting too much emphasis on hitting and too little on pitching. With another young arm to complement the "Human Slat," the Blues might have brought a pennant to Cleveland, but good young arms don't grow on trees.

Angry over their inability to capture first place, many of the players openly challenged natural rival Pittsburgh to meet them in a post-season series. The Blues claimed they were better than the 1903 National League champs and demanded a chance to prove it. The Pirates agreed to a five-game series, and the teams hired Bill Klem to umpire the games. Fans in the two cities anxiously waited for the games to begin. Cleveland rooters were delighted to have the chance to see the great Honus Wagner in person, in a head to head match-up with Larry Lajoie. Wagner brought with him a fine supporting cast, led by outfielders Fred Clarke and the National League's leading hit-getter, Ginger Beaumont.

Opening the series in Cleveland, the teams split two hard fought games. Addie started game three in Pittsburgh, holding the Pirates to one run over eight innings. In Cleveland's half of the ninth, Elmer Flick blasted a triple off the right center field fence, driving in two runs for a 3-1 advantage. Addie tried to wrap it up in the bottom of the ninth. With one out he worked carefully to Wagner, who fouled out to Harry Bemis. Pirate first baseman Kitty Bransfield topped a slow roller down the third base line. Bill Bradley charged the ball, picking it up and firing to first in one quick motion. Cleveland felt the throw got there in time, but Klem signaled safe, setting off a major argument from the Blues bench. Addie lost his concentration, surrendering three straight hits to send the game to extra innings. Cleveland threatened in the tenth, but left two stranded as Beaumont raced to the flag pole to haul in Bradley's long fly. That represented the last scoring threat either team could mount. Klem called the game after fourteen innings when darkness enveloped the field. The next morning brought an abrupt change in the October weather, prompting the teams to shorten the series to three games. Addie had spent himself pitching the previous day. Despite scattering fifteen hits, he managed to last a full fourteen innings, striking out eight and not giving up a single walk.

The Blues scored a victory in the final game, marred by rain and a swirling wind that sent chills through all in attendance.

From the bench, Addie and several other teammates hurled insults at Umpire Klem for his questionable safe call the previous day. At one point Klem called time, ambled to the Cleveland bench and warned Addie to shut up or be tossed from the park. Despite encouragement from fellow troublemakers, Addie went silent. Then Wagner started mouthing off at Klem from the other bench, which resulted in a quick exit for Hans. The victory in the shortened series removed some of the sting from Cleveland's poor season, but the pennant remained as elusive as ever.

Addie packed his bags for the trip back to Portage. Once again he spent the winter quietly, playing pinochle with Lillian and Theresa. After three successful seasons, he was content. However, during the winter he got a letter from Charles Somers offering him a bonus of $500 if he won twenty or more games in 1905. The challenge got his attention. He intended to win the bonus or blow out his arm trying.

Toledo's Sunday Sports Editor

PREPARING TO LEAVE FOR SPRING TRAINING, Addie learned that Larry Lajoie had been named player-manager of the team. Dashing "Nap" was popular with the fans, and Somers and Kilfoyl felt he would help the box office, while his fiery personality might shake the players out of their doldrums. The team almost immediately became known as the Naps, a nickname that would last as long as Lajoie remained manager.

One of Lajoie's first decisions sent the pitchers and catchers to Hot Springs, Arkansas for early workouts. The plan called for the mini-squad to assemble in the third week of February. Once there, the players were to take advantage of the warm water spas in combination with light pitching exercises. Lajoie hoped that the early start would get the pitchers into top shape in time for the regular camp in Atlanta, Georgia.

Addie checked in at Hot Springs bending the scales at 215 pounds. He made good use of the facilities, quickly dropping to a healthy 200. The players worked out at a field owned by the Pittsburgh Pirates. Left to their own devices, each man slowly brought himself into playing condition. After one day's practice, Addie walked to the post office to pick up a letter. He was initially baffled by the long line of men in front of him. He explained the scene to Henry Edwards when he arrived in Atlanta. "Well, when

I got there, I had to stand in line for nearly half an hour, there being fifty or sixty men ahead of me. Everyone had misery intermingled with hope stamped on his face. They were men that had gone broke on the races and were after letters with money that never came. While I stood there studying them, one or two were successful, and how their faces lighted up when they drew a check from the envelope. It certainly was pitiful."

As the Georgia training camp broke up, Addie decided to wear a bright red sweatshirt under his uniform for good luck. The idea belonged to new pitcher, Bob "Dusty" Rhoads, who convinced Addie to try the new wardrobe. It worked. Addie won nine of his first ten starts. On Memorial Day he recorded his first shutout of the year, beating St. Louis, 1-0. A single by Terry Turner scored Harry Bay with the game's only run. In addition to his pitching, Addie surprised the fourteen thousand fans by singling and stealing two bases.

Heading into June, the Naps grabbed first place behind Addie's strong pitching. He faced the White Sox, holding them to one run over nine innings. The game went into extra innings. Addie held the line through fifteen innings, not allowing a runner to reach second base. The Naps broke the game open in the top of the sixteenth, when a Turner triple scored both Lajoie and Flick. Bay singled to bring home Turner, giving the Naps a 4-1 advantage. Chicago scored a run in the bottom of the inning, but a quick double play ended the game, 4-2. The sixteen innings marked Addie's longest appearance in the major leagues.

The pressure of occupying first place tightened the nerves of the usually easygoing Cleveland players. It was at this time, on a trip to New York, that Addie fired his glove point blank at Umpire Silk O'Laughlin. With teammates restraining Addie to prevent a brawl, O'Laughlin ejected him from the field, sending him to the bus outside the grounds. Before order could be restored, catcher Fred Buelow got the thumb, as did New York's Clark Griffith. Ban Johnson ordered the five day suspension.

After missing one turn in the rotation, Addie shut out Washington, 2-0. He gave up three singles and allowed no runners to reach second base. In Philadelphia, he bested Waddell. After spotting the Athletics two runs in the first inning, the Naps tied the score, then took the lead, 3-2, in the top of the ninth when Addie scored on a sacrifice fly by Elmer Flick.

Returning home to Cleveland, the team stared in bewilderment at the crowd of over 10,000 waiting to greet them at the Euclid Avenue depot. When the train pulled to a stop the fans went into a frenzy, blowing horns and whistles. Nearby, tugboats blared their horns adding to the volume of the celebration. A band hired to serenade the players struck up the popular tune, "You Are as Welcome as the Flowers in May." To truly show their appreciation for the Naps's good showing, the crowd hired a fleet of carriages to transport the players back to their rooms at the Kennard House.

The day began with a joyous celebration, but finished in a fit of anger. That afternoon Addie pitched poorly, yielding eight runs in a lopsided loss to St. Louis. In the fourth inning the Browns catcher lifted a pop fly over the first base line. The ball had spin on it, landing in fair territory then twisting towards the foul line. Addie raced over, reaching down to pick up the ball. Before he got there the batter kicked the ball while running towards first. Addie motioned to Umpire Jack Sheridan that there had been interference and the runner should be out. Sheridan ruled the opposite, claiming Addie touched the ball with a finger while it was still fair. Frustrated later by some ball and strike calls, Addie yelled to Sheridan, "Great Scott, man, if you can see that good why don't you see some of those strikes that I'm putting over?" At the end of the game belligerent fans hurled hundreds of seat cushions onto the playing field.

Sporting a record of 12-2, Addie developed a severe head cold. He missed several starts while the Naps slid out of first place. Lajoie contracted blood poisoning from a spike wound, keeping him away from the game for a month. Various bumps and bruises caused the team to slip out of contention yet again. In late September Addie faced Detroit, needing only one more win to reach twenty. He surrendered three runs in the bottom of the first, the key hit being a single by rookie Ty Cobb. The Naps rallied for three runs to tie the game in the top of the eighth. In the Tiger half of the ninth inning Cobb led off with a ground ball to first baseman George Stovall, who booted it. A sacrifice moved him to second, then with two outs, Matty McIntyre grounded to Stovall who again could not find the handle. To the Naps's surprise, the young Cobb never stopped running, streaking across home plate with the winning run.

Addie got his twentieth victory on the final day of the season. He beat Detroit, 5-3, in spite of five errors committed behind him. The win was meaningless in the standings, but it meant $500 for the Joss family. Using the extra money, Addie purchased a house in Toledo, moving Lillian and Norman to Fulton Street, close by the downtown business district. By now he had accumulated an impressive list of friends including the mayor of Toledo, Brand Whitlock. Addie maintained ties with several of the Toledo sports-writers, often visiting the newsroom to talk baseball. The mayor regularly attended these sessions, sometimes bringing along an entourage of city officials. At times Addie dropped by the Mayor's office, answering sports questions posed by his honor and the police chief.

Addie enjoyed many close friends in Cleveland, as well. Bob Rhoads and Larry Lajoie were his best friends among the Naps. On rival teams, Addie developed friendships with Doc White and Ed Walsh of Chicago, and Cy Young of Boston. Some forty-five years later, Young, in his eighties, traveled to Milwaukee to accept a plaque for Addie's induction to the Wisconsin Sports Hall of Fame. Outside of baseball, Addie maintained a friendship with Ben Hopkins, a Cleveland businessman who developed an idea for a belt line railroad. The plan called for the laying of tracks around the city, enabling trains to stop at various plants and factories without traveling directly through the congested traffic of the city center. The plan succeeded, boosting Hopkins to an elite status in the business world. Despite his good fortune, Hopkins's first love was baseball. Every spring he visited the Naps's training camp, donning a uniform and working out with the team. In later years Hopkins displayed his regard for Addie, by using his influence

Addie, Lillian and Norman in 1905.

with Cleveland's upper crust to aid the Joss family.

In February, 1906, elated that Lillian was pregnant with their second child, Addie again departed for Hot Springs. In Arkansas he briefly attempted to learn the fadeaway pitch made famous by Christy Mathewson. Addie developed a good break on what we would now call a screwball, but did not feel the command necessary to use it in a game. He stuck to his fastball, curve, and changeup. He often threw his fastball as a ground-ball producing sinker, which was then sometimes called a "false rise." When all else failed, he brought out the heat, throwing a sidearm fastball with a hop on it. Record books list Addie as one of the top fielding pitchers in the history of the game, and he benefited through much of his career from a superior defense behind him. As a ground ball pitcher, he had the luxury of Bradley and Lajoie behind him. Terry Turner played an above average shortstop.

The 1906 season bore many similarities to the previous one. Cleveland started fast, seized possession of first place, then faltered when injuries took their toll. After two shutouts in his first three starts Addie found himself pitching more frequently than ever. In one seven day stretch, he appeared in four games, starting three and relieving in one. Lajoie made Addie his workhorse, sometimes giving him only two days off between starts. For three months the strategy kept the Naps in the hunt.

At the end of June, Addie readied himself to pitch on the road against Detroit. The previous day in Chicago, Herman "Germany" Schaefer had belted a game home run to stave off defeat for the Tigers. Schaefer, an eccentric famous for stealing first base, did not have a reputation for hitting the long ball. His feat did not go unrewarded as manager Armour gave him the start against the Naps. When Schaefer strode to the plate he received a raucous ovation from the Tiger backers. Addie knew all about the previous day's heroics, and prepared to quiet the crowd as quickly as possible. He proceeded to fan Germany four straight times, including the final out with a runner on first base. The *Plain Dealer* commented, "Herman Schaefer had a chance to show the fans just how he won the game at Chicago Sunday, but Dutch struck out."

All told, Addie fanned seven, allowed three hits and did not issue a base on balls. More important, he kept Ty Cobb off the bases. Addie had relative success against Cobb over the years, usually preventing him from dominating the game. The two adversaries offered an interesting match-up. Cobb displayed great intelligence as a batter, using all of the field to place his hits. He bunted when the opportunity arose and ran wild on the bases. He knew the strike zone. With his great control, Addie threw curves on the corners to Cobb. He held the Tigers star in check, and beat Detroit with regularity.

On July 18 the Naps were surprised when Jack Kilfoyl appeared unannounced in their New York hotel. Kilfoyl summoned the players for a short meeting. He explained that, as an incentive to win the American League pennant, both Charles Somers and he would add a total of $5,000 to the players' World Series receipts. With Kilfoyl watching from the stands, Addie demonstrated that money talks, shutting out the Highlanders, 5-0. In the second game of the scheduled doubleheader everything came apart. Bill Bradley took a high hard one directly on the right wrist. The pitch shattered the bone and sent him to the sidelines for the rest of the year. Soon, several other players were hurt, and Addie began to play center field when he wasn't pitching. To compound matters he developed a sore shoulder which caused him to miss several starts. Addie asked for permission to leave the team and travel to Toledo, where he arrived just in time for the birth of his daughter, Ruth Theresa. After a short visit, with mother and baby, he rejoined the Naps to pitch against Boston. Unable to throw fastballs or hard curves, Addie spotted the ball effectively enough to shut out Boston, 4-0.

For the year, the statistics read twenty-one victories against nine defeats. Nine shutouts represented an astonishing forty-two percent of his total wins, and his earned run average was 1.72. He again collected a $500 bonus.

While the Ohio weather stayed neutral, Bill Bradley's Boo Gang barnstormed around the upper regions of the state. In games scheduled west of Cleveland, Addie met the team to hold down an outfield position, while a Cleveland teenager named Richard Marquard did the pitching. The remaining four brothers of the late Ed Delahanty played on the Boo Gang, all of whom had appeared at one time or another in the major leagues. The extra money helped a bit, but Addie realized he needed to pick up a solid off-season income to support his family comfortably. He aired his regret at failing to complete his studies in civil engineering. With nothing to fall back on when his playing days ended, he racked his brains for an occupation outside the dugout. Looking at his peers in the game, he saw a variety of pursuits. The bigger names had the clout to take to the road on the vaudeville circuit. Stars such as Christy Mathewson, Ty Cobb, and later George Herman Ruth pulled in big dollars acting in plays or giving dramatic readings. Lesser names like Harry Bay earned a few hundred dollars a week touring the smaller cities with his wife and musicians. For Addie the thought of more time away from home had lost its appeal. He centered his efforts on the Toledo area, attempting to find a job that did not include any travel. A number of ballplayers had gone into retail businesses. Larry Lajoie operated his smoke shop, while Bill Bradley opened a sporting goods store. Astute ballplayers capitalized on their popularity with fans, drawing a customer base from men who regularly attended games and enjoyed mingling with their favorite stars.

Addie hit upon a different idea altogether. He approached the editors of the Toledo *News Bee* with the idea of writing a weekly column. Drawing on his own experiences over the last six years, he retained a vast resource of baseball stories and anecdotes. Though he had no journalistic experience, Addie had the best source of information available: himself. The *News Bee* editors were interested in Addie's idea, offering him a position as Sunday sports editor. His duties included putting together a full page of baseball stories, contributing much of the material himself. Fans starved for baseball during the off-season could be counted on to buy newspapers that contained features of the national pastime. The editors felt Addie's name would give circulation a good shot in the arm, making the venture a profitable one.

For his part, Addie kept a high profile in Toledo. He joined the Masons, taking pride in the hand-carved, ceremonial sword and ring. He continued to participate in the afternoon gatherings at the sports desk, eventually drawing large audiences to hear his views on baseball topics. Rubbing elbows with the Mayor and city politicians did not hurt Addie's status as the foremost baseball authority in town.

Weeks before the column debuted, the *News Bee* kicked off a campaign to draw attention to the paper's Sunday sports editor. It ran announcements on the front page proclaiming the virtues of its new columnist. The editors sought to create an air of excitement among their readers and potential new subscribers. In one of the editions, a cartoon appeared on page one depicting Addie in a baseball suit, flinging copy to an editor who donned a catcher's mask to protect himself from the steady flow of news hurtling his way. A batter stood near the editor, swinging wildly at the copy sailing past him. All in all the paper did a clever promotion, and the Sunday sports page proved to be a major success for all involved. Addie's bosses installed a private telephone line so that he could personally field the huge number of calls overwhelming the switchboard. The *News Bee* enjoyed increased profits, while Addie gained a reputation as a competent feature writer. He adopted the journalistic style of the day, relying heavily on the slang and popular phrases used by the sportswriters he knew and read. He did a good deal of research in preparation for his column, quoting names, dates, and places with regularity. The stories ranged from serious commentary to humorous yarns concerning past and present teammates. Addie paid attention to local baseball, devoting space to predictions on the Mud Hens and other minor league clubs in northwest Ohio.

Addie commenced his literary career with an opinion on the number of games scheduled for World Series competition. Charles Murphy, the owner of the Chicago Cubs, maintained that the current seven game format did not give the teams enough time to display their true talents. Addie wrote, "President Murphy of the Cubs brings forth the argument that a series of seven games for the world's baseball championship is too short to determine the ability of the contesting teams. Perhaps this was induced by the fact that the Cubs were beaten by the Sox in the 1906 championship. Everyone who follows baseball is aware that an important factor in baseball is the way the luck of the game breaks and it can readily be appreciated, that in a series of so few games, this will have much to do with the winning of the championship."

Addie owned a dry sense of humor that he sprinkled through his columns. His writing was lively, often inducing a chuckle or two. He strove to be entertaining, while providing the reader with the "inside dope" known only to the ballplayers, and he was successful.

In a feature about Cy Young, Addie responded to critics who maintained the Boston pitching star had seen his better days. He wrote, "Some people are under the impression that Denton has about outlived his usefulness, but should anyone with this impression happen to be at the plate sometime next July and see him whipping them through with the same old cannon ball speed and accuracy for which he is noted, most likely he would change his opinion." In fact, Young's brilliant career had assuredly reached its twilight stages. But Addie refused to concede that his good friend might be on the long slide down. He was still a ballplayer, and he was willing to skirt the truth to protect one of his fraternity.

Addie wisely devoted space to news of the hometown Mud Hens, taking an optimistic view of their prospects for the 1907 season. Since he had successfully weathered the storm of deserting Toledo only five years before, he had no inclination again to raise the ire of his friends and neighbors.

Moving away from pressing hot stove issues, Addie related some comical tales to his readers, particularly stories about current and past Naps. One of his favorites was about spring training, 1904. Red Donahue, sometimes known more for his wit than pitching ability, started an exhibition game against an amateur team from San Antonio. Being careful not to put any stress on his pitching arm, Donahue took a pounding from the local players. Addie described an exchange between an angry spectator and the ineffective pitcher. "Oh, Red, you are easy!" shouted the fan. Donahue turned slowly in the direction of the heckler. "Easy eh, well I ain't half as easy as you are, you gave up half a dollar to see me pitch today!"

Superstition played a significant role in the day-to-day preparation of the ballplayers and managers. Addie himself believed in his lucky red sweatshirt, and he also paid close attention to the number thirteen. When he was going good he tried to use a locker with that number, and when he was on the road he sometimes requested a room in the hotel that had thirteen in it. Addie explained to his readers that meeting a cross-eyed person the day of a game surely meant for a long afternoon. Bill Bradley spent much of his free time searching for cross-eyed boys and smuggling them on the playing field. Addie disclosed what would inevitably transpire. "Bradley once managed to find a small boy who was so cross-eyed that it was hard to decide whether he was coming or going. 'Brad' knew Armour was on the bench and he sent the kid in with instructions to ask Armour if he wanted a good mascot. The boy did as he was told and when Bill saw those eyes he nearly fell off the bench." Addie maintained a load of barrels or hay represented a definite sign of good fortune. He told readers that players on their way to the ballpark were on the lookout for barrels, and if they sighted any would raise their hats in unison, saluting the clear sign of victory.

The Sunday sports page served as a springboard for Addie's newfound occupation. A Brooklyn newspaper offered him a winter job writing a weekly column. Much closer to home, the Cleveland *Press* contracted with Addie to cover the 1907 World Series as a special correspondent. The paper also hired him to write features for the following winter. Addie gradually came to feel, probably correctly, that he had a solid career to turn to when his playing days were over. For now, though, he was pleased that his new Sunday page was a success, and that another spring training waited just around the corner.

The Holdout

IN JANUARY, ADDIE RECEIVED HIS CONTRACT for the 1907 season. It called for a salary of $3,100, good money for the time, and a $400 raise over the previous year's base. But the $500 bonus for winning twenty games was not included, so even if Addie had a very good season, his income would be $100 lower than in 1906.

Stung, Addie returned the contract unsigned and advised Somers and Kilfoyl that he would not report unless they increased their offer. The owners chose not to respond, feeling Addie would change his mind by the February 2 reporting date for pitchers and catchers. Somers and Kilfoyl knew that the players were bound by the reserve clause, and couldn't simply offer their services elsewhere. They could only withhold their services, in the hopes that the team would feel that it needed them. There had never been a successful holdout under the current regime.

In this instance, Addie gave notice he intended to fight it out for the duration. Using his power as sports editor, he publicly announced his holdout in the Sunday sports page. He wrote, "I have not heard anything from Cleveland and will stick right here in Toledo. I haven't been in communication with the club and therefore do not know what I am going to do. This holdout business is something new for me, but I am not bluffing." When the story broke all the Cleveland papers picked up on it, fanning the flames even higher. The *Plain Dealer* carried a story that Addie and Bob Rhoads were in collusion to jointly force Somers and Kilfoyl to improve their contracts. Addie refuted the allegation, stating to the press, "There is no combination between Rhoads and myself. We are not trying to hold up the club."

While both sides mulled the situation over, the *Plain Dealer's* Henry Edwards phoned Addie at his Toledo home. Hoping to clarify his position Addie told the reporter, "I merely ask to be paid what I am worth as a baseball pitcher. I led the righthanders of the league last season and feel that I should at least get as much as I did during the season of 1906." Being able to plead his case in the papers aided Addie's cause greatly. Public sentiment ran high in his favor, and letters to the papers supported his stance. They called for the Cleveland owners to give in before things escalated and the Naps's hope for a pennant were dashed. The Cleveland *Press* announced they were conducting a poll on the holdout. Fans were invited to mail in their vote with any comments they felt appropriate. The *Press* counted over 600 responses, with the huge majority in Addie's favor. In an attempt to deflect the criticism, Jack Kilfoyl explained the owners position. He pointed to Addie's lack of durability, never appearing in more than thirty-two games in a season. Based on the number of games he had pitched, the owners felt that $3,100 was generous. Kilfoyl concluded by saying that it was inappropriate to discuss player salaries in public. From this point on there would be no further comment.

As the second week of March approached, the situation remained unchanged. The *News Bee* announced Addie would continue the Sunday sports page for as long as the standoff lasted. The editors loved the holdout because of the added interest it brought to the newspaper. On March 8, Henry Edwards decided to try to mediate. He again phoned Addie, asking him if he would be willing to take a train to Cleveland to meet with his adversaries. Receiving a positive response, Edwards visited Somers and Kilfoyl to get their approval for a conference. With both sides consenting, a meeting for eleven o'clock on the morning of March 9 was set. Addie caught the 6:50 train out of Toledo, packing a grip in case of a settlement. The parties met for thirty minutes while reporters anxiously waited outside the offices. When the doors opened all were smiling. Addie signed a new contract for $4,000. At twelve noon the Toledo *News Bee* received a telegram stating, "Signed. Terms O.K.—Add."

In all his years with Cleveland, 1907 was the only year Addie had a contract dispute. He had a history, of course, of stubbornly pursuing what he considered a good deal. He left Juneau for Wayland, and Wayland for Sacred Heart, each time furthering his career and improving his remuneration. He "struck" to force the strapped Oshkosh owners to pay him. He signed with Cleveland when he knew Toledo had at least a reasonable claim to his services. And he knew what he was worth after a few years with the Naps. Addie was generous, but he was tough about the money he was paid because it reflected his value as a player. In the pinch, he was unwilling to compromise. This calm certainty under pressure may also help to explain why he was such a "money" pitcher.

Traveling direct to training camp in Macon, Georgia, Addie proceeded to destroy belief in the one-month sojourn in Hot Springs. He pitched effectively from the start, displaying no soreness in his arm. He held a clinic for the hurlers from Mercer College, which Henry Edwards named, "The Joss Institute of Twirlology." The most interesting news item from camp was a trade that didn't happen. Charles Somers received a surprise phone call from Hughie Jennings. The Tigers manager, weary of Ty Cobb's disruptive attitude, offered to swap the young star for veteran Elmer Flick. Somers declined. Flick, at thirty-one showed no signs of slowing down, and the Cleveland owner worried that Cobb might upset the chemistry of his team. The trade, of course, might have brought the pennant to Cleveland, and it would have brought the city the dominant player of his generation.

Somers had no way of foreseeing that injuries and illness would end the careers of Flick and Harry Bay by the end of the 1908 season, by which time Cobb had led Detroit into two World Series. But he can reasonably be faulted for not recognizing the sheer ferocious genius in Cobb's game. Somers would never win a pennant.

On the journey back to Cleveland, the team made a stop in Toledo to play an exhibition against the Mud Hens. Addie twisted manager Lajoie's arm for the chance to pitch the April 7 game. This represented Addie's first appearance in Armory Park since the fall of 1901. Despite a driving rainstorm that lasted until game time, Addie stepped on the field in front of a capacity crowd numbering in excess of 5,500. Some of the crowd had to stand on the soggy ground behind ropes strung across center field. In the top of the first, the visiting Naps erupted for six runs. Addie walked to the mound, trying to conceal his excitement beneath the vast crowd's thunderous ovation.

Pitching five strong innings, Addie gave the Mud Hens a healthy dose of major league hurling. At the bottom of the second inning, a group of fans strode to the mound to present him with an appropriate gift: an umbrella. After the game he spent the evening at home, visiting with his family.

Addie began the regular season with a flourish, winning his first ten starts. After an opening day win at St. Louis, he returned to League Park to face Detroit. Entering the top of the seventh the Tigers had failed to produce a hit. Up in the press box, the reporters, as superstitious as the players, avoided mentioning the word, no-hitter. A young boy in the crowd, not yet initiated into the superstitions of the game, yelled audibly, "Guess Joss is going to pitch a no-hitter!" Sam Crawford promptly lined a single to right. An error and a hit batsman loaded the bases with none out. Addie walked Germany Schaefer, forcing in a run. He got Charlie Schmidt to ground to third, where Bill Bradley threw home to get the force. A pop out and long fly ended the inning. Cleveland won the game, 4-1. It was Addie's third one-hitter.

Pitching effectively, Addie suddenly found his batting eye as well. In a struggle against the St. Louis Browns, neither team had scored going into the bottom of the seventh inning. With two men on base and two out Addie smashed a deep drive off the right field bleachers, scoring both runners. He tried to stretch the hit to a triple, but the relay from the outfield caught him at third base. Winded by the long sprint, he grabbed the water bucket for a big

Addie in his prime.

swallow. He choked on the drink, swallowing his wad of tobacco. This brought on a fit of coughing, which turned his skin a light shade of green. The Naps gathered around Addie, laughing at his dilemma. After a few minutes he returned to the mound to win, 2-0.

Addie's proved his batting heroics were no fluke, singling in the winning run against Boston. Near the end of May he beat Waddell and the Athletics, 5-2, for his tenth straight victory, claiming a Cleveland pitching record. With this win, the Naps climbed to second place, just one game back of the world champion Chicago White Sox.

Cleveland fan interest in Addie's win streak ran high. Hours before his next start against Detroit, thousands of Clevelanders lined up outside the ticket gate. They kept coming, forcing the ticket office to close its windows, turning away another 1,000 spectators. The ticket count read 17,316, one of the largest crowds ever seen at League Park. The overflow pushed the players off their benches, forcing them to sit on the grass several feet from the foul lines. Addie brought out his red sweatshirt, trying to muster all the help he could get. The Tigers paid little attention to the massive crowd or lucky sweatshirt, touching up Addie for three runs in the top of the first. The crowning blow came in the second, when Cobb slammed a tremendous home run high over the right field wall. The ball came to rest on Lexington Avenue while the crowd watched dumbfounded. Detroit took advantage of six Nap errors to stop the Joss streak at ten.

Despite some improbable circumstances, Addie continued to pitch impressively. In a matchup with Ed Walsh and the White Sox, the players waited on the field only to be informed that the League office had blundered in assigning an umpire to work the game. Rather than postpone the game, both sides agreed to have substitutes handle the umpiring duties. For an inning the informal arrangement worked, but in the top of the second all hell broke loose. With a runner on second and none out, Chicago's Patsy Dougherty blooped a single to left field. The runner rounded third and headed for home. The throw arrived in time to nail him. However, Chicago's designated umpire, pitcher Nick Altrock, stood in back of the mound, watching Dougherty advance towards second. He wheeled around too late to see the play at the plate. Altrock gave the safe signal, touching off a wild argument from players and irate fans. When order was finally restored, the game continued without incident. The final score read: White Sox 2, Naps 1. The disputed run at the plate accounted for the difference in the game. The Cleveland front office protested the contest, collecting signed affidavits from all the sportswriters in the press box. The documents were forwarded to Ban Johnson to support the protest. The Naps waited for weeks for Johnson to respond, but he refused to issue any ruling on the matter, and the score stood.

Rolling into July Addie kept up his hot pitching, tossing three straight shutouts against Chicago, New York, and Boston. He ran up twenty-nine innings of scoreless ball until Philadelphia pushed across a run to break the streak. This produced the famous Joss temper tantrum, where Addie threw to first while nobody covered the bag.

Lajoie told sportswriters that if his pitcher could keep up the pace, the Naps just might bring the pennant home to Cleveland. Trailing the leaders by only percentage points gave hope to the anxious Cleveland followers. At the beginning of August, Addie had posted eighteen wins and only six defeats in keeping the Naps close to the top.

The strains of a real pennant race slowly unraveled the Cleveland team. While the players lounged around the lobby of their Philadelphia hotel, a local fan questioned Lajoie on some managerial decisions. First baseman George Stovall resented the fan's questions, demanding that Lajoie tell off the inquiring fan. That prompted a heated discussion between player and manager, culminating in a $50 fine for Stovall. After more angry words, Stovall grabbed a heavy oak chair and flung it at Lajoie. The flying chair missed its target, but Lajoie suspended Stovall immediately. The next morning infielder Frank Delahanty arrived at the ballpark seemingly intoxicated. Lajoie suspended him as well, sending the two offenders back to Cleveland ahead of the team. Angry over the incidents and anticipating another collapse, Charles Somers announced he had enough, offering the team for sale. Nobody came forward and Somers quickly rescinded the offer, keeping control of the franchise for years to come.

To the surprise of many, the Naps did not fold, staying close to front running Detroit. When the Tigers came to town on "Lajoie Day," Addie stood ready to slow them down. After a lengthy cere-mony for the manager's thirty-second birthday, Addie took care of business, retiring the first seventeen batters before pitcher Ed Killian stroked a single. The only other Tiger to reach first base was Cobb, who drew a base on balls. In the fifth inning Addie brought the crowd to its feet by striking out the Tiger outfielder. Since Cobb's controversial collision with Harry Bemis, the Cleveland fans delighted in razzing Tyrus every chance they got. The next day, in an effort to make amends, Cobb flipped a ball into the right field seats, which temporarily quieted the fans. The Naps won, 3-0, behind Addie's fourth one-hitter. He struck out eight, six in the last five innings. Commenting on the performance, Lajoie said, "There is not another pitcher living who has anything on the big fellow when he is right, and he was right today."

Unable to close the gap with Detroit, Addie still pitched out-standing ball. He ended the season with his third one-hitter of the year, defeating New York, 3-1. The run scored on a two base error and sacrifice fly. For the season, Addie led the major leagues with twenty-seven wins. He had the American League's second-best winning percentage, and stood third in complete games and earned run average. He accounted for nearly a third of Cleveland's eighty-five wins. He did not miss a single pitching turn all season. A Chicago newspaper ran a story on Addie that pretty well described the Cleveland situation. "Addie Joss is a wonder and if Cleveland had two more of him, they could begin spending the money of the world's championship series now, that is of course with Charlie Murphy's permission. The Cubs might object. But there is only one Joss on the Cleveland team and he can't pitch every day."

Addie traded in his pitcher's glove for a fountain pen, traveling to Chicago to report on the Detroit-Chicago World Series. The day before the series started, the Cleveland *Press* ran a headline announcing their coverage of the games. They stated, "Of all the baseball players in the land, Addie Joss is far and away the best qualified for this work. A scholarly man; an entertaining writer; an impartial observer of the game; the readers of the *Press* will be assured of reports of thrilling interest."

Surrounded by the cream of the crop in sportswriters, Addie received a fast course in sports journalism. As a member of the press corps he got some real insights in the daily routine of reporting baseball games. In his three years of covering the World Series he developed a style all his own, and became more of a writer covering baseball than a ballplayer giving his impressions. In a later year, Addie colorfully described the afternoon practice in Detroit. "A tremendous throng cheered the Tigers to the echo as they ambled gracefully out on the field for practice this afternoon, preliminary to the fourth game with the Chicago Cubs for the world's championship. After the victory of the Tigers yesterday at Chicago, the most faint-hearted fan in the bunch plucked up courage and saw a chance for the bird of victory to perch on Detroit's roost."

Addie's game summaries were picked up by United Press and syndicated across the country. The writer was becoming as well known as the ballplayer. This pleased Addie, but he still had one big goal left to reach, one that had proven to be the most elusive of all—pitching the Cleveland Naps to the World Series.

The Great Pennant Race

PROSPECTS FOR CLEVELAND TO BE A FACTOR in the 1908 pennant chase seemed slim at best. The pitching staff of Joss, Rhoads, Liebhardt, and Berger combined for a total of 215 career wins. Addie himself accounted for 118 of those, while Bob Rhoads totaled seventy-four. To say the pitching lacked depth was a major understatement. The defensive alignment matched the early 1902 squad, which include a lineup of nondescript players destined for obscurity. Of course, Lajoie still manned second base, while Stovall and Bradley held down the corners. George Perring played shortstop in place of the injured Terry Turner. Elmer Flick had a serious stomach problem, lost twenty pounds, and couldn't play all season, so the outfield featured light hitting Josh Clarke (Fred's brother), Joe Birmingham, and Bill Hinchman, who showed some power, but paled in comparison to the man he replaced. The reigning champion Tigers boasted the great outfield of Cobb, Crawford, and Davy Jones, and their pitching staff was strong and experienced.

Sportswriters felt Cleveland had little chance for a successful season, picking the team to finish sixth or worse. Chicago figured to be in the thick of things along with Detroit and possibly New York. No one had any kind of inkling that the 1908 pennant race would be one of the greatest of all time, or that the Naps would make a spectacular September run that would propel them right into the middle of it. While the blood pressure of many a fan rose to critical levels, Detroit, Chicago, and Cleveland battled down to the season's final outs. To keep the Naps fighting for their chance to win it all, one pitcher put forth an effort that has yet to be surpassed. He dug deep inside for the sheer heart and determination that carried him to new highs as a ballplayer. He came within an eyelash of pulling off a miracle. In 1908 Addie Joss truly became king of the pitchers.

After spring training, Cleveland once again journeyed north to Toledo for its traditional exhibition. Addie fared much better than he had the previous year, receiving gifts of roses, a silver cigarette case, a traveling outfit, and a pair of handsome diamond cuff links. It now became clear why Addie insisted upon pitching the game. He knew he stood to make out like a bandit from his local well-wishers.

Three days later he pitched the home opener, losing a ten-inning struggle to St. Louis, 2-1. Addie's wild pitch in the top of the tenth paved the way for the Browns to plate the winning run. From that point on, Addie duplicated his pitching record of 1907, reeling off ten straight victories. The highlight of the streak took place at home against the Tigers on April 28. In the top of the third with Detroit leading, 4-2, manager Lajoie called on Addie in relief. He struck out the first hitter he faced, but Harry Bemis mishandled the pitch, allowing the runner on third to cross the plate. Addie got the next two batters to end the inning with Cleveland behind, 5-2. The Naps fought back in their half of the inning, scoring once and loading the bases. That brought Addie up to hit amidst audible groans from the patrons in the grandstand. His batting record for the young season was abysmal. Expecting the worst, fans winced when Addie took a big cut at the ball. To the amazement of all, he made contact, driving the ball to deep right center. The blast cleared the bases and gave Cleveland the lead. Addie pulled up at third with a stand-up triple. Leading off the sixth, the Naps's new hitting star lined the ball down the left field line for a double. Three runs scored in the inning, putting

Cleveland comfortably ahead, 9-5. To cap things off, Addie belted his second double of the game in the seventh inning. He tried a delayed steal, but took off too early and was retired. The Naps won, 11-5, with Addie pitching six and two-thirds innings without allowing an earned run. He struck out four, did not walk a man, and totaled five assists during his stint. At the plate he chalked up a triple and two doubles, driving in three runs including the game winner. In honor of his winning performance, members of city council who were in attendance sent Addie a large bouquet of flowers. He refused them. "Give them to someone that has deserved them," he said. "Yes, I pitched some ball and batted some but did you see me make that bum effort to pull off the delayed steal? Rotten? Well I guess it was. It was the limit." Later he forgot about the bum effort and called the game the most satisfying of his career.

Addie's win streak continued through May. Playing in New York, neither side scored through seven innings. Bill Hinchman singled in the Nap half of inning number eight. With one out Addie went deep to center field, driving Hinchman home with his second triple of the year. The Naps were victorious 2-0. The Highlanders managed just three hits, only one of them leaving the infield.

On June 3, Detroit stopped Addie's win streak at ten games for the second year in a row. The Tigers scored in the bottom of the ninth to defeat Cleveland 2-1. Addie hurt his arm, missing several starts while the Naps slid behind the leaders. By the end of August, Cleveland held down fourth place, trailing Detroit, the surprising St. Louis Browns, and the Chicago White Sox. Going on past history, Nap supporters felt there was no chance that their team would make any noise in the stretch.

On September 1, Addie pitched the sixth one-hitter of his career, beating Detroit 1-0. Ty Cobb's single in the first inning accounted for the Tigers's only hit. After losing to the White Sox, Addie came back two days later to shut them out on two singles. He did not allow a runner to reach second base. Four days later he won again, placing the Naps only one percentage point out of third place.

Cleveland fans suddenly realized that their team had begun a move. Once again large crowds of fans gathered outside the Plain Dealer offices to wait for the scores. The newspaper began to run game summaries on the front page, gradually creating a state of frenzy which escalated throughout September. Lesser knowns such as Heine Berger and Glen Liebhardt contributed stellar performances, while newly acquired Wilbur Goode lit up American League pitching. Each game a different player captured the limelight with a clutch hit or pitching performance.

Standings – September 11, 1908

	W	L	Pct.
Detroit	75	53	.586
Chicago	73	57	.562
St. Louis	71	58	.550
Cleveland	72	59	.549

Now that the pennant had drawn within reach, Addie turned up his performance a large notch forward. On September 17 he faced old nemesis Cy Young and the Boston Red Sox. The two mainstays dueled for eight innings, neither allowing a run to score. While a highly anxious crowd waited for a break, Addie retired the side in the top of the ninth. Bill Hinchman, now the Naps's hottest hitter, led off the home half with a single. Lajoie followed with a bunt, legging it out for a single as the ancient Young could not reach the ball in time. The Boston infield moved in towards home, expecting another bunt to move the runners over. George Stovall swung away, lining the ball past the drawn in infield. Hinchman lumbered around third to score the winning run.

Standings – September 17, 1908

	W	L	Pct.
Detroit	78	56	.582
Cleveland	78	60	.565
Chicago	76	61	.555
St. Louis	72	59	.549

This game marked Addie's fourth straight win down the stretch, his third shutout of the month. The Naps climbed into second place, only four games behind Detroit in the loss column.

The next day Bob Rhoads pitched the game of his life, throwing a no-hitter against the Red Sox. To sweeten the experience, New York defeated Detroit, tightening the race by one full game. Three days later the unthinkable occurred. Detroit lost and the Naps posted another victory, taking sole possession of first place. On September 22, Addie won his fifth straight game, throwing yet another shutout to beat New York. A bases loaded single by Harry Bemis broke the game open as Cleveland pushed across seven runs for an easy win. Only ten percentage points separated the top three teams.

Standings – September 22, 1908

	W	L	Pct.
Cleveland	82	60	.577
Detroit	79	60	.568
Chicago	80	61	.567

In his last twenty-seven innings Addie had allowed only a single run. He had completely dominated the likes of Speaker, Crawford, and Cobb. His September wins included a one-hitter and a two-hitter and four shutouts.

Detroit did not falter. The veteran Tigers were eager to atone for their performance in the 1907 World Series against the Chicago Cubs. In spite of the spirited play of Cleveland, the Tigers kept pace, defending their league crown like true champions. The White Sox kept up the pressure behind the phenomenal pitching of Ed Walsh. The spitballing righthander was in the midst of a career season, flirting with a forty win season. No strangers to pressure, the world champions of 1906 made a stubborn effort to overtake the Naps and Tigers. None of the three contenders could pull away from the pack, and none faded. The race would be down to the wire.

Five days later the Naps fell out of first place, trailing Detroit by a percentage point. Chicago tightened the gap, closing to within a half game of second. At month's end the three teams still stood together. The American League scheduling committee had unknowingly heightened the drama by its pairing of teams for the final week of the season. Over the winter they had matched the Naps and White Sox for two, then the Naps at St. Louis for the final three while Chicago finished at home with three against Detroit. The Tigers hosted tough

Standings – October 1, 1908

	W	L	Pct.
Detroit	87	61	.588
Cleveland	87	62	.584
Chicago	85	62	.578

fourth-place St. Louis before going to Chicago to end the regular season. The Browns, enjoying their finest season since 1902, relished the idea of playing spoiler with either Detroit or Cleveland.

On Friday October 2, the final desperate hours of the pennant race commenced. The Cleveland management moved the start time up to two-thirty, to ensure that there would be enough daylight in case of extra innings. The weather forecast called for clear skies with temperatures in the fifties. No rain. Hours early, fans began to file in to League Park, far too excited to wait until the contest began. Spectators milled around the field. Many wore business suits, while others were in shirt sleeves and bow ties. All the men wore hats. Cigar and cigarette smoke rose around the park. Many women attended, forming groups of rooters that kept together without the escort of husbands or suitors. The women rooted as hard as anyone, providing the Naps with faithful support.

In the grandstand, men strung lines of cowbells across poles. Many fans carried horns and whistles. Jack Kilfoyl sat in his owner's box anxiously waiting for the game to begin. He teetered on the brink of nervous exhaustion. The strain of watching the Naps fight tooth and nail for the pennant had pushed him to the brink of collapse. After each late season game, he arrived home unable to compose himself for hours. He would soon divest himself of his interest in the team, selling out before his health deteriorated any further.

Although Lajoie did not announce his starting pitcher until game day, every fan in the city knew Addie would be the man. The White Sox countered with Ed Walsh, setting the stage for a duel between the American League's two best hurlers. Big Ed had his spitball working to perfection, while Addie had not lost a game in nearly a month. It promised to be a battle of epic proportions.

Minutes before game time, Addie finished his warm-ups, taking a stroll around the field. He noticed Walsh, bat in hand, sitting quietly on the visitors bench. He walked over to his opponent, joining him on the bench for some idle talk. At that moment a photographer snapped their picture, capturing an image of two friends having a quiet conversation. The picture stood in stark contrast to the circumstances about to unfold on that crisp fall afternoon. It would be the only calm moment for the next several days.

At precisely two-thirty, Addie walked to the mound oblivious to the huge roar from the ten thousand vocal spectators, most of whom had skipped out of work early to witness the struggle. He took his final warm-ups, concentrating on leadoff hitter, Ed Hahn. He put them down in order, setting the tone for the remainder of the game. Walsh took up the gauntlet, fanning the Naps's leadoff man, Wilbur Goode. Cleveland went down quietly, giving an indication that this game would be won or lost on the pitcher's mound. Addie realized early that Walsh had his good stuff with him. To win the game he had to hold the line, hoping for a run to work with. He too, had his pitches and his control working for him. Addie set down nine straight batters without the semblance of a hit.

Joe Birmingham started the Nap half of the third by singling to

October 2, 1908. Under immense pressure near the end of one of the game's great pennant races, Ed Walsh and Addie Joss share a quiet moment before taking the mound against each other. Walsh was spectacular. Joss was perfect.

right for the game's first hit. Though not a prolific base stealer, "Birmy" ran well enough to draw Walsh's attention. He slowly edged away from first base, getting a big lead from the bag. Quick as a cat, Walsh pivoted toward first, firing the ball to Frank Isbell. The throw caught Birmingham leaning, and he took off toward second. Isbell's throw to the shortstop plunked Birmingham in the back. While the crowd screamed, the ball bounced into center field, and Birmy went into third standing. George Perring bounced out to short, with Birmingham holding at third. With one out Addie stepped to the plate and feebly tried to lay down a bunt. Three waves at the ball produced out number two. With Birmingham creeping down the line, Walsh struck out Wilbur Goode. But Walsh and substitute catcher Ossee Schreckengost, a former Bluebird, got their signals crossed, and the ball sailed out of the catcher's reach. Schreckengost made a desperate stab at the pitch with his bare hand, smashing a finger in the process. Birmingham scored easily, putting the Naps one up.

Using the gift run to full advantage, Addie bore down even harder on the White Sox batters. His pitches were low and away or inside under the wrists, shaving the corners of the plate. In the fourth, all three batters hit at Lajoie, while in the fifth Addie fielded two grounders after striking out the leadoff man. All the outs were routine except a high chopper that Addie grabbed on the third base line and threw to first. The White Sox had yet to put anything in play that resembled a base hit. Walsh for his part pitched beautifully, keeping the Naps well back on their heels. He struck out a steady procession of Cleveland hitters, nearly two per inning. Lajoie fanned twice, and Wilbur Goode four times.

Entering the seventh, the realization took hold that no Chicago batter had reached first base. A drama within a drama began to unfold among the nervous crowd. Winning the game was absolutely vital, but interest began to shift toward the potential perfect game. Sportswriters observed men throughout the grandstand holding unlit cigars, completely oblivious to anything except what was happening on the field. The cow bells hung silent, and the hundreds of horns and whistles were mute. One writer noted that a pin drop could be heard across the stands. Writers spoke in hushed tones, worried that any kind of distraction might jinx the game. Telegraph operators from Chicago, Detroit, St. Louis, and New York signaled through the wires for constant updates. The same question repeated itself again and again. "Hasn't anyone reached first?" The Cleveland operators feared a response to the requests would break Addie's string. "Wait!" they wired back. "Wait till the end of the game!"

With one out in the seventh, player-manager Fielder Jones stepped up to the plate, determined to break the spell. He crowded the plate, working the count to three balls and one strike. Addie fired a fastball over the plate for strike two. At that instant, ten thousand lungs seemingly sucked in all the oxygen around the park as they waited for Addie's next delivery. Slowly he lifted his arms above his head, turning toward second. He uncoiled to home, shooting a sidearm curve under Jones's wrists. The umpire never hesitated, raising his right arm to indicate strike three. Jones argued vehemently,before stalking back to the bench talking to himself. A ground ball to Lajoie ended the inning.

Addie walked slowly back to the bench, noticing his teammates were avoiding him. He sat alone, softly rapping his knuckles on the wooden bench for good luck. He figured nobody would dare speak to him. He hoped for another run or two, but acknowledged the tremendous effort put out by Ed Walsh. He resigned himself to the fact that one run would be all he had to work with.

In the top of the eighth, Chicago's Patsy Dougherty rapped a hard ground ball at Lajoie. The ball took a bad hop, but the manager stayed with it, grabbing the ball in front of his eyes, and flipping to Stovall. A pop fly to Lajoie, and a routine fly to Bill Hinchman ended the Sox portion of the inning. Joe Birmingham got his second hit of the game, but died at third while Wilbur Goode fanned for the last time. Over eight innings, Walsh had recorded fifteen strikeouts, which broke the American League record. He allowed four singles, walked one, and was charged with the wild pitch that let in the Naps lone tally.

It hardly seemed like four o'clock when Addie finished his

warm-ups to start the ninth. For most, the time had gone excru-ciatingly slowly. Now with three outs to go, the fans cheered silently for Addie to finish it off. Fielder Jones refused to go quietly, sending a succession of pinch hitters to the plate. Doc White, one of the few good hitting pitchers in the game, faced Addie from the left side of the plate. He got a piece of the ball, pulling it towards the ever busy Lajoie. Larry scooped up the ground ball and flipped to Stovall for his eighth assist of the day. Jones called on another lefty, first baseman Jiggs Donahue to be the second pinch hitter. Addie showed no signs of fatigue, striking out the White Sox hitter on three straight pitches. Donahue swung hard at each one, failing to make contact.

Down to the final out, Jones pointed to John Anderson to grab a bat and get out there. The switch hitting Anderson had been around various teams for fourteen seasons. At the end of his career, he could still swing the bat. He chose to hit from the right side of the plate, which alerted Bill Bradley to guard the line at third. Bradley later explained that he expected Anderson to try and pull the ball, so he moved close to the bag, guessing he might have a play. As if scripted Anderson drove the ball right at Bradley, who made the stop. He fired the long throw to Stovall a bit low, but the first baseman reacted quickly, reaching in the dirt to make the pickup. Umpire Silk O'Laughlin shot his right arm in the air, signaling the game's final out. Within seconds the crowd let go with an explosion of noise which some claimed could be heard ten blocks away. Hundreds made a dash for Addie, hoping to carry him around the park. Seeing the wild throng rushing toward him, Addie turned and sprinted for the clubhouse behind center field. He clocked record time, arriving inside before the delirious fans reached him. While he was trying to catch his breath, reporters fought their way to his locker, demanding to know what it felt like. Addie calmly replied to their questions, "I did not try for such a record. All I was doing was trying to beat Chicago for the game meant much to us and Walsh was pitching the game of his life. I never saw him have so much." He then made sure to mention the support behind him. "Don't forget the boys played grandly, while

Larry (Lajoie) killed three drives that would have been hits for ordinary second baseman." Ed Walsh took the loss in stride, giving credit to Addie's effort. "I am sorry we lost of course, but seeing that we did have to lose, I am glad that Addie took down a record that goes to so few. I guess way down in my heart I was sort of glad when 'Silk' called Anderson out in the ninth. It would have made no difference anyway."

A man named Peter Witt had brought a registering device to the game. For his own enjoyment, he decided to track the number of pitches thrown. At the end of the game his machine recorded seventy-four pitches thrown by Addie, an average of just 2.74 per batter.

As Addie stated to the writers, this game was vital to the Naps. And it took the performance of a lifetime to win it. Taken as the climax of his superb September, Addie's perfect game was the icing on the cake of the greatest sustained clutch pitching display in the game's history.

Although there were four games yet to be played, fans poured out of the park carrying on as if the pennant had been secured. Shopkeepers, merchants, doctors, and lawyers came running out of their shops and offices to learn what they'd missed. Lexington and Dunham were filled with celebrants, singing and dancing well into the evening hours. Most showed no concern that Detroit had beaten St. Louis or that the White Sox had still one more game in which to settle the score.

On Saturday afternoon, in front of a record crowd, the Naps fell behind, 3-2. With two outs in the seventh, they loaded the bases, bringing Lajoie to the plate. Fielder Jones waved in iron Ed Walsh to face Cleveland's premier hitter. The strategy worked to perfection as Walsh crossed up Lajoie with a two-strike fastball to retire the side. Two more scoreless innings by Walsh and Chicago had squared the short but vital series. Detroit had won again in St. Louis. The players dressed quickly, hustling to catch a five o'clock train to St. Louis. Each man knew nothing less than a sweep of the final three games would do. The Tigers needed to win two of three, regardless of what the Naps did to clinch the flag. By taking three straight from Detroit, Chicago had a chance to win the flag, depending on how Cleveland fared with St. Louis.

Early Sunday morning, the Naps arrived at the St. Louis train station, filing out of the cars to catch a fleet of cabs to their hotel. Addie was walking slowly through the depot when he suddenly pitched forward in a dead faint. Shocked teammates gathered around, and he regained consciousness in less than a minute. He struggled to his feet, refusing to see a doctor or stop at the hospital for an exam. He did not appear to be ill, leading to speculation that he suffered from exhaustion. There were doubts that he would be able to start either Monday or Tuesday. The fainting spell was soon forgotten until several years later when Addie collapsed again, this time during spring training.

Bob Rhoads started Sunday's game, quickly surrendering three runs. In the bottom of the fifth, Lajoie sent Heine Berger in to replace Rhoads. The change only made things worse as Berger walked the first hitter on four pitches. A sacrifice moved the runner to second. Berger continued to be wild, walking the next batter to put runners on first and second. Desperate and feeling the season slipping away, Lajoie motioned to Addie to warm up.

Addie had time to throw only four or five tosses when Lajoie waved him to the mound. He threw two balls to Danny Hoffman, completing a walk begun by Berger and loading the bases for Dode Criss. The Browns had failed in their attempt to slow down the Tigers, but they still wanted to play a role in the pennant race by beating Cleveland. The crowd smelled blood. Addie got ahead in the count, then jammed Criss with a curve, forcing a pop fly which Bill Bradley handled in fair territory. He then fanned Jimmy Williams on three straight pitches to bail the Naps out of trouble. Addie held the Browns's bats silent for the balance of the game, and Cleveland clawed back to tie. With one out in the top of the ninth Addie drew a walk. A fly out held him at first, but Bill Bradley doubled into the gap in left center, putting runners at second and third. Bill Hinchman next drove the ball past the pitcher's mound. Just inches away from the outfield grass, shortstop Bobby Wallace dove headlong and knocked it down with his glove hand. He scrambled to his knees and fired the ball to first. Hinchman crossed the bag, seemingly beating the throw. Addie scored and Bradley rounded third, making a try for home. Tom Jones, the St. Louis first baseman, raced toward the line, cutting off Bradley and forcing him to dive back to third. At that instant first base umpire Jack Egan surprised everyone by indicating that Hinchman was out and Addie's run didn't count. The Naps erupted, charging Egan and demanding he change his call. The fact that Jones, who would know better than anyone if the runner had crossed first safely, chased Bradley back to third, proved to them that Egan had erred. After the game, Jones told sportswriters that he felt Hinchman had beaten the throw.

Addie set down the Browns in order in the bottom of the ninth, sending the game to extra innings. Aware that darkness was rapidly becoming a factor, Cleveland made a bid to end the game. Lajoie led off with a double, advancing to third on George Stovall's second hit. The Browns moved their infielders in to cut off the run at the plate. Catcher Nig Clarke bounced to Jones, who looked Lajoie back to third before forcing Clarke. Joe Birmingham fouled out to the catcher. With everything at stake, George Perring drilled a line drive that Bobby Wallace snagged to end the threat. The Naps had blown a golden opportunity to win the game and had precious little time to stage another rally. Addie pitched quickly, keeping the Browns from scoring through inning number eleven. But daylight faded toward darkness, leaving the umpires with no choice but to suspend the game. It would be replayed on Monday.

Cleveland's last chance to gain on Detroit slipped away in the twilight. Chicago had beaten the Tigers, but the Naps had wasted Addie's superb relief stint, and lost the chance to gain a full game. The controversial call by Jack Egan was a factor, but the inability to get Lajoie home with nobody out was the final blow to Cleveland's championship hopes.

Addie had nothing left to offer for Monday's doubleheader or Tuesday's finale. He had given the Naps two outstanding games in forty-eight hours. In fifteen and two-thirds innings, Addie did not allow a run, gave up two hits, and issued one walk, that coming in relief with the count two balls and no strikes. He did everything possible to bring home a championship.

A 3-1 loss Monday morning ended all hopes for glory. Cleveland won their final game to clinch second place behind Detroit. Their ninety wins left them a half-game short. Addie won twenty-four games, lost twelve, and led both leagues with an earned run average of 1.16. He allowed only thirty bases on balls in 325 innings, less than one per game. No other pitcher could match that. He averaged less than seven hits per game, second only to Mordecai Brown of the National League Cubs. The most impressive aspect of Addie's season was his record of 7-1 through September and October. Five of the wins were shutouts, including the perfect game. He nearly pushing his Naps to the pinnacle of success. The fainting spell suggests he may have given too much. He never approached this level of play again.

Addie left St. Louis for Detroit to begin his coverage of the World Series. Now a veteran reporter, he blended in well with the beat writers. His features were indistinguishable from those of the seasoned pros. After the Cubs won their second straight championship, Addie made the short journey home to Toledo, where he wrote columns for the *News Bee* and the Cleveland *Press*. Pushed time and again to explain why the Naps failed to win the pennant, he finally devoted a feature to answering that question. Ignoring all else, Addie sighted the October 3 loss to Chicago as the deciding factor. He pointed to several missed opportunities in that game that ultimately cost the Naps their chance at post season play. This had to be the biggest disappointment of Addie's career. There would be no more chances at the pennant.

Disappointment and Injury

ALONG WITH HIS JOURNALISM, Addie turned to other ways to make extra income. At the time, inventing and endorsing baseball products was evolving into a popular vocation among players. It allowed them to make off-season money without barnstorming or vaudeville. Lajoie introduced a model bat with his name on it. Cy Young developed and endorsed a type of chest protector. Elmer Flick invented a new style of sliding pad, and not to be outdone, Bill Bradley created an infielder's glove that he displayed at his sporting goods store. Addie joined the crowd and marketed an oil for baseball gloves.

He also dusted off his civil engineering books, studying for an idea that he planned to propose to Somers and Kilfoyl. He knew that fans had trouble keeping track of balls and strikes, and that many of them couldn't easily see the score. He designed, in essence, an electric scoreboard. He drew up plans to build metal numbers twenty inches high so they could be easily seen from any point in the park. The club bought the Joss Indicator, placing it on a new, larger, scoreboard which featured the batting lineups on either side of the balls and strikes. Posting the player lineups came through the urgings of Ban Johnson, who wanted all the parks to adopt the idea. Somers and Kilfoyl were the first. Addie revealed to curious reporters that he had built a small, handheld device that could post strikes on the board from the pitching mound. Based on his performance in 1909, it is safe to say the device malfunctioned.

Packing up the family, Addie met the advance squad of pitchers and catchers in Mobile, Alabama to start spring practice. When time permitted, Addie took his wife and kids on sightseeing jaunts around the city. Norman attended all workouts, usually getting in some batting practice, with Dad doing the pitching. Many remarked the six-year-old rivaled his father as a hitter. During a scrimmage, Addie stroked a line drive to center field which went for an easy out. While trotting back to the bench, Norman observed loudly, "Pa, that would have been a great hit you made if the man hadn't caught it!" The players cracked up, watching Addie shake his head and grin. The Joss party remained at Mobile for a month, savoring the extended vacation. When camp broke, Addie rode with them to Toledo, then caught a train to St. Louis to pitch the season opener. Based on their play of the previous year, the Naps were touted to be one of the favorites to finish in first place. Charles Somers evidently felt the same way, for he failed to make any significant changes to the roster, with the exception of forty-two-year-old Cy Young and new catcher Ted Easterly. As the team stood pat, other clubs revamped their rosters to remain competitive. Connie Mack built a new infield led by Eddie Collins and Frank Baker. He added pitcher Jack Coombs to his staff, combining him with veterans Eddie Plank and Chief Bender. Boston unveiled a new outfield featuring Harry Hooper with the great Tris Speaker. Their pitching staff received a boost with teenager Joe Wood and young Eddie Cicotte. Detroit still boasted the best one-two punch in the league, Ty Cobb and Sam Crawford. Cleveland did not match up well with the American League's fresh talent, falling backward all the way to sixth place, eleven games under .500.

Addie experienced his first losing season as a professional, finishing with a record of thirteen wins and fourteen defeats. After winning the opener against St. Louis, he returned to Cleveland to pitch the inaugural game. The Browns belted him all over the field, forcing him out of the game after four innings. He seemed to regain his form in a short time, tossing a one hit shutout over the youthful Philadelphia Athletics, 2-0. Addie put together a string of victories, peaking at six in a row. The highlight of the streak came again at the expense of the Athletics. He went ten innings, allowing only two hits in a 1-0 nailbiter. By mid-July, he owned a record of eleven wins versus three losses, seemingly on pace to another twenty-win season. In August Addie hurt his back, possibly during a playful wrestling match with one of the Naps. When he returned to the rotation, he had lost his effectiveness, at times being removed for a relief pitcher. The team collapsed by the end of summer. Lajoie grew increasingly frustrated, and tendered his resignation as manager. He returned to his chores as player only, tired of the double duty he had held for nearly five years.

In September, Addie reached a milestone in his major league career. While being shelled by the Tigers he slammed a long home run to the right center field seats, his first and only round-tripper with the Naps. He took some solace in Ty Cobb's comments in the Cleveland *Press*. Ty named him the hardest pitcher to hit in the American League. The Tiger star said, "Addie can put a curveball exactly where a batter can't hit it nine times out of ten."

But in 1909 the ball wasn't going exactly where Addie threw it. He spent most of September on the bench, watching a steady progression of new recruits try out for the team. He pitched only 242 innings all season. His earned run average again stood below two, at 1.71. And for the second year in a row he led both leagues in fewest walks per game at 1.15. But he didn't win.

In Addie's defense, the Naps were a shadow of the team that finished so strong the previous year. The good defense and timely hitting Addie benefited from vanished completely in 1909. Still, Cy Young somehow managed to win nineteen games, sporting the only pitching record on the team above .500.

Arriving in Pittsburgh for the start of the World Series, Addie wrote about the high prices scalpers were demanding. His first dispatch to the Cleveland Press read, "Speculators have obtained no such large blocks of tickets as they were able to secure in Chicago last fall, but men and boys holding from two to six tickets were sprinkled among the crowd, demanding from $10 to $20 each for the coveted pasteboards. It is on record that an offer was made at the Hotel Schenley of $160 for eight tickets in a row." He noted that hundreds of fans slept outside the ticket gates for a chance to buy general admission seats the morning of the game.

Back home in Toledo, Addie accepted an offer to tour Cuba with a group of major league players. Most of the roster came from the National League, with the world champion Pirates sending three players and the Cubs represented by Jimmy Archer and Artie Hofman. Fred Merkle made the trip, as did one representative each from Philadelphia, Brooklyn and Boston, all from the National League. To help with the pitching duties, reports mentioned Nap Rucker, Howie Camnitz, and Mordecai Brown joining the squad for its December 1 departure. Hank O'Day served as the umpire for the schedule of twelve games. The Cuban teams gave the Americans all they could handle, whipping the heavy favorites on several occasions. The sketchy press reports criticized the All-Stars, rather than acknowledge the caliber of competition. Addie lost one game, 2-1, on a ninth-inning home run.

During the early months of 1910, stories circulated that Addie had gone past his prime as a pitcher. They cited not just his disappointing 1909 season, but his losing performance in Cuba. The fact that Addie struck out eleven batters and had a shutout going for eight-plus innings in his 2-1 loss did not appear in any of the criticism.

Whether a coincidence or not, Addie traveled to Hot Springs on his own in 1910, to get an early jump on spring training. He found enough players there to form two teams for scrimmages. The extra work helped him get in shape when he joined the Cleveland squad in Alexandria, Louisiana. He pitched three shutouts in March, quieting the criticism against him.

After winning the season's opener despite giving up seven runs, Addie started an April 20 contest at Chicago. In the bottom of the second, Fred Parent hit a ground ball down the third base line. Bill Bradley juggled the ball, dropped it, then picked it up, throwing to first a half step late to get Parent. The official scorer hesitated with the call, first announcing hit, then changing his decision to error. His ruling took on significance as the White Sox struggled to get a hit. Addie picked up a whopping ten assists, fielding every ball hit his way and making the toss to first. Only three balls were hit out of the infield. Cleveland scored its lone run on a double in the sixth inning by Terry Turner. For the second time in his career, Addie registered a no hit, no run game, claiming the White Sox again as his victims. Still fretting about his decision, the official scorer wired the Cleveland papers, explaining his reasons for giving Bradley an error. Evidently he had drawn some heat in the press box for not giving a single to Parent, thus helping Addie to his no-hitter. This was eight years almost to the day after the controversial call in St. Louis left Addie with a one-hitter in his debut start.

Cleveland returned home to take part in the ceremonies at the rebuilt League Park. At a cost of $300,000, the wooden stands had been torn down and replaced by a structure of concrete and steel. The park now held 21,000 spectators and had twenty-six exits to allow for the larger crowds the owners were anticipating. At two-thirty the players marched to center field for the raising of the stars and stripes on the new flagpole. Ban Johnson threw out the first ball in front of a crowd that included most of the American League's club owners and about 1,000 factory workers whose plants had shut down in honor of the event.

Addie followed up his no-hit effort with some inspired pitching for the next several weeks. He chalked up four wins before a twelve-inning 1-1 curfew game stopped his streak of wins. His first loss came against Walter Johnson and the Senators, a 1-0 decision. Three singles in the home half of the first accounted for the game's only offense. Both pitchers mowed down the hitters for the balance of the game in a spirited duel.

On June 5, Addie admitted to having a problem with his right elbow. He didn't reveal when or how the injury occurred, but he noted a sharp pain with swelling after he pitched. He took his regular turn four days later, and was hit hard by Philadelphia in a 4-4 tie. The Athletics pounded Addie freely, belting out twelve hits over eight innings. After the game he had his elbow examined. The diagnosis was a torn ligament. The treatment called for complete rest over the next month. Addie left the team to scout some minor league prospects for manager Deacon McGuire . On July 11 he tested the elbow, beating Boston, 5-4. But he couldn't throw the sharp breaking stuff without a shooting pain up and down his arm. He could not survive on his fastball alone and he knew it. When the team left Boston, Addie remained in town to be treated by a specialist. The same doctor had helped Eddie Cicotte recover from arm problems. In between visits, Addie scouted New England teams. He left for Philadelphia after a week of treatment, unsure if his arm felt any different. On July 25 he gutted out five innings against the Athletics, but he had to leave the mound when the elbow swelled up again. This was his last regular season appearance.

In Cleveland, Addie visited the office of Dr. Morrison Castle, the team physician. After a thorough exam, the doctor advised him to go home and completely rest the arm for the rest of the season. He reluctantly packed his grip and left for Toledo. He rented a cottage in Sandusky, a popular resort area off Lake Erie. While the children played on the sandy beaches Addie pondered his baseball future, wondering if he was finished. Fourteen years of throwing sidearm breaking balls had put a huge strain on the elbow. If indeed there were torn ligaments or muscles, there was no way in those days to correct the problem. Rest relieved the pain and swelling, but it did not heal the injury.

News of a postseason series between Cleveland and Cincinnati reached the Toledo papers. Unable to wait for the upcoming spring, Addie wired McGuire asking for permission to pitch one of the games. Receiving a favorable response, he arrived in Cleveland to start on October 13. When he walked to the mound, the fans greeted him like a long lost friend. The sportswriters did not know Addie had returned, contributing to the drama of the moment. For five innings the clock turned back to previous glories. Addie let go with everything he had, holding the Reds to two scattered hits. In the sixth he ran out of steam, allowing two runs to score. Taking a seat on the bench, he watched his team win easily, 5-3. Though tired, Addie felt little pain in his arm, and this gave him some hope that his elbow might be healing after all. He confided to Henry Edwards after the game, "I think I will enjoy my best night's sleep tonight I have had in several months. Yes, I had a nice rest at my summer cottage but there never was a night when I did not lay there and wonder if my arm had gone back on me for good and if I ever would be able to pitch again. It was a tough summer for me and I don't want to go through another, not just yet."

In the winter months, Addie got himself involved in multiple business ventures. He declined to write his usual sports column, opting instead to buy a half interest in a billiard parlor. His business partner was Abe Holt, a veteran billiard hall operator in and around Toledo. The combination of Addie's great popularity and Holt's skill at turning a profit resulted in a fairly lucrative establishment. Their location downtown in the St. Paul building offered easy access to businessmen seeking a beer and a quick game of billiards before calling it a day. Addie put in his share of hours at the parlor, greeting old friends and acquaintances in addition to tending bar and wielding a mop when necessary. He handled a cue stick quite well, accepting challenges from any and all comers.

Urged on by Doc White, Addie finally agreed to venture out on the vaudeville circuit over the winter. He joined a quartet, featuring White and two members of the Chicago Cubs, Artie Hofman and Jimmy Sheckard. The Keith circuit tour began November 14 in Chicago. Nothing is known about audience reaction to the singing ballplayers, but Addie returned to Toledo without any severe injuries.

When he wasn't working at the billiard parlor, Addie looked up old friends George Mullin and Roger Bresnahan, all Toledo residents. The three did a little clowning around together, playing some practical jokes in which Bresnahan was often the victim. Bresnahan was employed as a private detective in the off-season. One evening Addie, gasping for breath, telephoned the St. Louis player-manager to tell him that he and Mullin had been out walking and had spotted a dead body. Bresnahan rushed over, and ran with the two witnesses to a downtown location. Addie and Mullin pointed upward to a stairwell, imploring Bresnahan to climb the steps and check out the corpse. In the darkness, Bresnahan had not realized the stairwell led to the county morgue. He dashed up the steps until he heard the laughter behind him, finally figuring out he'd been had.

The arrival of Cleveland trainer Doc White put an end to Addie's free time. The club wanted to be certain of Addie's services for 1911. Charles Somers sent White to Toledo with instructions to work on the arm twice a day for as long as it took to heal. Every morning at eight o'clock and every evening at six, White called on Addie at Fulton Street to administer treatment. The trainer suspected a torn ligament above the elbow accounted for the pain and swelling, which made the arm useless. White manipulated the injured arm, actually causing the swelling to reappear. He termed the condition "natural soreness," which would wear off in a couple of weeks. Addie was encouraged with the prognosis, and decided to travel to Hot Springs to bathe the arm in the warm baths. He told the newspapers he would be ready to pitch when the season began.

With time to kill before spring, Addie made the rounds at the Toledo *News Bee*, providing quotes and giving his opinion on Cleveland's chances for the new season. Always the optimist, he predicted big things for his ballclub, feeling an influx of young players like Joe Jackson would revitalize the team. He continued to work at his billiard parlor, happy to talk baseball with his patrons. Well into the cold and flu season, he labored long hours at the business, dodging coughs and sneezes from contagious men in the crowded rooms. In late February, Addie abruptly lost his appetite, dropping a good chunk of weight in a short time. He did not appear to be ill, going about his daily routine as usual. But Lillian made a point to mention the sudden change in appetite to trainer White.

In March Addie regained a portion of his appetite, leaving for Louisiana to prepare for the season. He worked out on his own, trying to bring his arm around without doing further damage. On a warm, sunny morning he decided to cut loose with everything he had. For twenty minutes he let go with fastballs and sidearm curves, holding nothing back. Initially he felt fine with the workout. The arm seemed to handle the all-out stress without any inkling of trouble. The next day while sitting on the bench, the old pain reappeared, shooting up and down the elbow. All the treatments administered by Doc White had failed to strengthen the arm. Frustrated, Addie told the Cleveland Press he had absolutely no clue what was causing the problem. He explained, "One day my arm feels great and the next day it hurts. I've tried every way I know to find out except the X-ray. I'm going to try that next week." Consistent with his optimistic nature, he told reporters he expected to pitch again by late April or the first part of May.

Tragic Finish

MONDAY AFTERNOON, April 3, brought the Cleveland team north to Chattanooga, Tennessee, for a game against the Lookouts. The weather in the south had heated up, featuring scorching temperatures and sweltering humidity. Addie stepped out of the clubhouse, peering at the huge fireball anchored above the field. He spied Rudy Hulswitt, an old friend recently with the St. Louis Cardinals. Addie sauntered over to the Lookouts's shortstop to catch up on recent gossip. Suddenly, he lurched forward, collapsing in the arms of the startled Hulswitt. Players raced over and carried Addie to the stifling clubhouse. Addie remained unconscious, breathing raggedly, and a frantic call went out for an ambulance. At the hospital, Addie revived, able to sit up and breathe normally. The doctors diagnosed heat prostration and let him check out of the hospital that evening to catch the team train to Cincinnati.

On the train, Addie began to experience chest pains. He changed trains, and headed for Toledo to see his personal physician, Dr. George Chapman. Chapman believed Addie, who had lost his appetite and was losing weight rapidly, was suffering from an attack of nervous indigestion or possibly ptomaine poisoning. Having been away from town for a month, Addie decided at the end of the week to take a stroll down to the *News Bee*. Staff members were shocked. He was slurring his words, and his cheeks were deeply sunken. He was clearly a very sick man. Nonetheless, Addie flashed his easy smile and assured his friends he would be all right soon.

On Sunday, April 9, Addie met with Charles Somers, who was in town for a game. He told his boss that he needed to rest at home for a time before rejoining the team. He next decided to call Dr. Chapman for another exam. The doctor this time diagnosed Addie with a severe attack of pleurisy. Speaking to the *News Bee*, Dr. Chapman announced, "Joss has a congestion in his right lung with a bad attack of pleurisy. He is not in danger, but uncomfortably ill. He is unable to draw a breath without severe pain." Pleurisy is described in medical dictionaries as inflammation of the pleura membrane lining the lungs and chest cavity. Its main symptom is chest pain that sharpens with each breath. He advised Addie to remain at home for ten days and forget about baseball for at least a month. Dr. Chapman overlooked other key symptoms, particularly the reduced appetite and sudden weight loss, which are possible symptoms of tuberculosis.

Addie's condition quickly grew worse. New complaints of a severe headache and constant coughing indicated to Dr. Chapman that the illness could not be pleurisy. He placed a long-distance call to team doctor, Morrison Castle, in Cleveland, asking him to come to Toledo at once. After informing Charles Somers of the situation, Dr. Castle hastily caught a train, arriving at Addie's home late Wednesday evening. He conducted his exam Thursday morning, April 13, noting Addie's headache, which continued to cause intense pain. He performed a lumbar puncture, carefully removing fluid from Addie's spinal cord, and analyzing it under a microscope. While the doctor studied the fluid, Addie walked around the house, saying to Lillian, "Gee Momma! My head aches!" He must have known he was seriously ill, but he tried to conceal his condition from his children, laughing and talking with Norman and Ruth.

Possibly the last photo taken of Addie Joss, 1910.

PHOTO COURTESY THE JOSS FAMILY

Dr. Castle shared his findings with Dr. Chapman. The diagnosis was tubercular meningitis. The original infection must have taken place weeks before Addie's collapse in Chattanooga, probably in early March. Tuberculosis is often passed by way of a cough or sneeze by an infected person. Addie had spent much of his time at the billiard parlor, and it's likely that he breathed the bacteria into his lungs there. It is common for the symptoms to lie dormant for a while. The fainting spell in Chattanooga, along with the loss of appetite and weight signaled the early stages of tuberculosis.

In Addie's case, the bacteria traveled to the base of his brain and triggered an inflammation of the membranes surrounding the brain. This is meningitis, and it was the cause of the severe headaches. In 1911, there was no cure, and no hope. All Dr. Castle could do was administer opiates to relieve Addie's pain while Theresa Joss was summoned from Portage.

Addie drifted in and out of consciousness. At about 1:45 a.m. on Friday, April, 14, 1911, Addie opened his eyes, mumbled to the nurse at his bedside, and in seconds was dead. It was just two days after his thirty-first birthday. Theresa Joss arrived at Fulton Street later in the morning, unaware of what had happened. She hurried up the walk only to see the black wreath hanging from the front door.

Over the next few days some news stories made reference to the fact that Addie's overall health and physical condition had been deteriorating for several years. One reported that he had had a serious bout with pleurisy two years earlier. Other stories claimed that the meningitis was brought on by overwork and exhaustion. In 1910, former Mud Hens manager Bob Gilks had given an interview to a Milwaukee newspaper. Either Gilks spoke tongue in cheek or he had thrown down a few too many brews before he talked to the reporter. He recalled that Addie reported to the Mud Hens weighing less than 150 pounds and that, because of his lack of bulk, he could pitch only two or three inning before he wore down. Gilks claimed he took Addie to a doctor for help, and that the pitcher gained enough strength by his second year to pitch complete games. But box scores show that Addie finished virtually all his starts as a member of the Toledo Mud Hens and missed very few turns on the mound. Addie was tall and thin—the Human Slat—but at six-foot-three he weighed 185 pounds when he joined Cleveland, only two years after he supposedly tipped the scales at under 150.

Gilks's tale was one of those baseball stories that are demonstrably unlikely, but gain credence in the face of facts. Since it received widespread distribution a year before Addie died, many fans in an era long before television believed the pitcher to be naturally frail, even sickly. Toss in vague memories of the fainting incident in 1908, and many believed that Addie just did not have the strength to fight off illness. In truth, Addie had the strength, grit, stamina, and spectacular good health of almost all great athletes. He also had the very bad luck to be in the wrong place at the wrong time, and to be infected with tuberculosis. When the bacteria entered his bloodstream and reached the base of his brain, he was doomed. To put it in layman's terms, he got the worst dose of what an already very serious disease had to offer.

Through the early morning hours, telegraph lines across the country burned with the news of Addie's death. Morning newspapers furiously scrambled to get the story into Friday's editions. Fans and friends reacted with shock, because few had any inkling that he had been seriously ill. The outpouring of public grief was unprecedented for an athlete.

Terry Turner marched out of the elevator of the St. Louis hotel lobby, ready to enjoy a hearty breakfast. A grim Deacon McGuire told him the terrible news, and asked him to tell the rest of the team when they arrived for breakfast. One by one each player learned of the death, and they gathered in small groups to quietly talk of Addie. George Stovall turned around and went back to his room, unable to speak to anyone. Later he expressed his thoughts to the reporters milling about the lobby. "It seems that I have lost a brother. No better man ever lived than Addie. His death has been a shock to us that we will not soon forget." Lajoie was the next to speak. He said, "In Joss' death, baseball loses one of the best pitchers and men that has ever been identified with the game. I am feeling very glum that my friend and teammate is no more."

From the American League office in Chicago, President Ban Johnson issued a statement. "His dear ones at home in Toledo, the Cleveland club and baseball in general has suffered a big loss in the death of Addie Joss. He was the kind of player who worked for the betterment of the sport and whom it always was a pleasure to see pitch, as his heart and soul were always in his work." These were eloquent words, but Johnson would soon have harsher comments for the Cleveland players.

The homage paid to Addie was not confined to the baseball community. Toledo mayor Brand Whitlock commented, "Most people will think of Addie Joss as a great baseball player, one of the greatest of his time. While he was that and that is a big thing to be, he was much more than that. He was as good a man as he was a pitcher, as good a husband as good a father, as good a friend, as good a citizen."

While the tributes continued to flow in, arrangements were made for Addie's funeral on Monday, April 17. Billy Sunday was conducting revival meetings in the Toledo area, and Lillian asked him to deliver a eulogy on Addie's behalf. The service would be at the Masonic temple.

Throughout the hours of Friday afternoon, wagon after wagon arrived at the Joss home to deliver floral arrangements. Among the first deliveries was a huge spray of red roses from Mr. and Mrs. Charles Somers. John I. Taylor, owner of the Boston Red Sox, sent a mammoth wreath of pink roses arranged on an easel. Teams from all parts of the country sent wreaths and arrangements to Toledo. The St. Paul team, in Toledo to play the Mud Hens, had a nine-string harp of white Easter lilies specially designed, with the last string broken to symbolize Addie's death. The White Sox sent a six-foot hamper filled with a vast assortment of flowers. Other arrangements of note included a three-and-a-half foot wreath from Mayor Whitlock and a basket of red tulips sent by Mr. and Mrs. Ty

Cobb. By late afternoon, Lillian had no room to accept more deliveries, having filled the porch until there barely existed a pathway for visitors to squeeze through. Old friend and former manager, Bill Armour, in his capacity as president of the Mud Hens, lowered the flag to half-mast at Swayne Field (the former Armory Park).

Telegrams of condolence arrived all afternoon and evening. Ex-teammates, now scattered around the country, wrote words of sympathy. The Cobbs's wired, "Please accept our deepest sympathies in your present bereavement. The shock was terrible to us. He numbered his friends by his acquaintances. We cannot find words to express feelings as we should." A decade later, as manager of the Tigers, he offered a tryout to Norman Joss. (Though a pretty fair pitcher, Norman declined, settling on an accounting career instead.) There is no record of any special friendship between the bitter, driven Georgian and the open, friendly pitcher, but Cobb at the very least seemed to have held Addie in high esteem.

Friday evening in St. Louis, several of the older Cleveland players met with Deacon McGuire to ask that the Monday game in Detroit be canceled so that the team as a whole could attend Addie's funeral. McGuire carried the players wishes to Charles Somers, who readily agreed. He phoned Tiger President Frank Navin, to ask for postponement of the game. Navin at first agreed, then wavered. A story circulated that manager Hugh Jennings talked Navin out of canceling the game. Jennings is said to have argued against setting a precedent for postponing games due to the death of players. Whatever the truth, Navin referred the matter to Ban Johnson, who emphatically stated the game would go on.

When they learned of Johnson's decision, the emotionally drained Cleveland players assembled in George Stovall's room to discuss their response. With Lajoie, Birmingham, and Stovall in the lead, a petition was drawn up, stating in effect that the team would not play baseball on Monday. The veterans pressured every player on the squad to sign, and Stovall, the team captain, handed the petition to a surprised Deacon McGuire. McGuire, who wanted to avoid problems with the powerful league president, chastised Stovall for failing in his duties as team captain. Reporters were close enough to hear Stovall reply, "I may be captain, but I'm still a ballplayer."

McGuire huddled with Cleveland vice-president, E.S. Barnard, and the two looked the petition over carefully. Birmingham spotted them in the lobby and marched over. Speaking in a clear voice, he said, "You don't need to worry about the handwriting and try to figure out whose it is, because it's mine."

When Charlie Somers learned of the player revolt on Sunday, he implored Johnson to change his position. Rumors had circulated that the Detroit players backed the petition, and would join Addie's teammates in not suiting up on Monday. Convinced the players meant to strike, the iron-fisted president, who had never backed down before, averted a public relations disaster by magnanimously calling off the game. A special train left St. Louis Sunday evening, bringing the Cleveland team to Toledo. Cars waited at the train station to transport the players directly to the Masonic temple.

On the clear, crisp morning of April 17, a horse-drawn hearse arrived quietly in front of the Joss house. At eleven o'clock a delegation of Masonic Knights Templar entered the house, lifted the casket and gently placed it in the hearse. A half-mile procession of automobiles and carriages wound its way through the downtown streets. The city and its businesses virtually closed down for the funeral, and the entourage passed thousands of mourners lining the curbs, men removing their hats as the hearse passed by. Over 15,000 more waited to pay their last respects at the temple. At noon the Knights Templar carried Addie's body inside, where it lay in state until two o'clock. An honor guard of Templars stood at attention at the foot of the casket, relieved every ten minutes by a fresh guard. The line of mourners, including delegations from Cleveland, other northeastern Ohio cities, and groups from Wisconsin, extended for blocks. Businessmen and laborers stood side by side, each waiting for a moment to say good-bye.

At two o'clock, Reverend Hollington offered a prayer, and then surrendered the podium to Billy Sunday. Surrounded by dozens of floral arrangements, the famed evangelist began his tribute. His voice rose as he spoke, "Joss was one of the great athletes of the world because he was a king in the game of baseball, and that is acknowledged as the star game everywhere. He was one of the men who, by his gentlemanly manner, sterling manhood, and unimpeachable honesty was an honor to the profession. He was one of those men who by their character and manhood have helped the game maintain its hold on the American people, from the President in the White House to the newsboy on the streets, from the staid and dignified members of the Supreme Court to the huckster, selling his wares from a wagon."

Taking his oration to another level, Sunday described Addie's last hours as a pitcher's battle against the specter of death. By today's standards Sunday's metaphors seem almost comical, but they touched the heartstrings of his audience. "Joss tried hard to strike out death, and it seemed for a time as though he would win. The bases were full. The score was a tie, with two out. Thousands, yes, millions in a nation's grandstand and bleachers sat breathlessly watching the conflict. The great twirler stood erect in the box. Death walked to the plate."

Sunday could not help but notice the tears and sobs among the congregation. His message drove home the finality of the moment. Many gave into their emotions, crying unashamedly. He described two pitches as balls one and two, setting the stage for Addie's last gasp. He proceeded, "Again the ball sped plateward. Addie's eyes became glassy, his muscles weakened, his mind failed. Ball three rang faintly in his ears. It was then that the great manager of the universe took the star Nap twirler out of the box and sent him to the club house." Sunday paused, and moved slowly to a position directly above the casket. He slowly raised his hand over Addie's face. His voice lowered to a whisper as he said his final farewell,

"Good-bye, Addie." Reporters noted that the Cleveland players in their seats wept uncontrollably. Their friend, their brother, was gone.

The service concluded with the Scottish Rite ring ceremony. In complete silence, the ring was removed from Addie's finger and presented to Lillian to be kept in trust for Norman. Once again the Knights Templar carried the casket to the hearse for the trip to Woodlawn Cemetery. The procession, including the Cleveland players, made its way to Addie's final resting place. After a brief service, the casket was placed in a vault for burial the following spring. A monument marked simply, "Joss" marked the burial site. For many years to come, the city of Toledo would vividly remember the day Addie Joss' remains were laid to rest.

A Fitting Tribute

AT THE TIME OF HIS DEATH, Addie's salary with Cleveland was $5,500. By 1911 standards the Joss family lived a comfortable life. But Addie, like his father, had neglected to take the time to compose a will, and Lillian had to deal with the probate court to sort out her late husband's estate. Despite the assets Addie left behind, Lillian realized the necessity of going to work to keep the family in a stable environment.

While Lillian worried about the future, Charles Somers was working to put together a benefit game for the Joss family. Such games were a long-standing tradition in baseball. Two years earlier, the A's had raised money this way in Philadelphia for the family of deceased catcher, Mike Powers. Somers wanted to arrange the greatest benefit ever seen, with some of the greatest players of the American League playing an exhibition game against the Cleveland club. He selected Monday, July 24 as the game date, because all the American League clubs except Chicago and Boston had the day off.

Somers heard from many civic leaders who expressed their interest in paying more than the regular price to attend the game. The club happily announced all box and reserve seats were available above face value, for people wishing to donate to the Joss family fund. Ben Hopkins accepted the responsibility of chairing the committee to solicit ticket sales from business and industry leaders. To get the ball rolling, Somers bought a ticket for his own private box at $100. Money began to pour in. The Cleveland Athletic Club raised $150 for reserved seats, topping the efforts of the Cleveland Elks who kicked in $100. Many businesses and organizations donated anywhere from $25 to $100. Individuals mailed checks for box and reserved seats, some of the donors preferring to remain anonymous. Hopkins added his own check for $25, matching the contribution of sportswriter Henry Edwards and Dr. Morrison Castle.

Players and owners from around baseball also sent contributions. New York, Boston, St. Louis, and Washington passed the hat to raise a total of $350. Charles Comiskey added $100, Ben Shibe sent $25, and National League owners Gary Herrmann and Charles Ebbets mailed $25 apiece. The Cleveland players bought $130 worth of tickets, Cy Young himself added $25 to the total, and Ty Cobb mailed a check for $100, equal to the greatest amount offered by any individual owner or team pool. Cobb wired instructions to Vice President Barnard to please keep his name out of the papers. Barnard phoned Cobb and convinced the Tiger star to change his mind, on the grounds that the mention of his generosity could only help boost donations. Cobb also committed to play in the game, though invitations had yet to be formally sent.

In keeping with the spirit of the benefit game, *Baseball Magazine* announced all sales during the afternoon of the 24th would be donated to the Joss fund. The employees of League Park declared their decision to work without pay as their contribution to the festivities. The final advance purchase went for $50 to Mrs. Frank DeHaas Robison, the wife of the former Cleveland owner and builder of the original League Park, who had ruined the Cleveland National League franchise in the late 1890s. Perhaps hoping to mend some fences, Mrs. Robison bought her seat.

With the financial aspects of the benefit well in hand, efforts shifted to bringing in the league's finest players. Outfielder Sam Crawford was asked to accompany teammate Cobb. Other invitations were sent to second baseman Eddie Collins and third baseman Frank Baker of Philadelphia; first baseman Hal Chase and pitcher Russell Ford of New York; shortstop Bobby Wallace of St. Louis, and pitcher Walter Johnson, catcher Gabby Street, and outfielder Clyde Milan of the Washington Senators. All accepted. Johnson wired, "I'll do anything they want for Addie Joss' family," Johnson said. "He was a player we all admired and there is nothing that any of us would not do along the lines asked. We will work our heads off to give the spectators some good sport."

To augment the roster, outfielder Tris Speaker and pitcher Joe Wood asked for and got permission to skip their game with Chicago to appear at League Park. The Red Sox stars told organizers that they could play the first three innings before they had to leave to catch a train for Boston. Catcher Paddy Livingston of the A's would accompany Collins and Baker. And Jimmy McAleer, Cleveland's manager in 1901, who had moved on to the Browns and was now Washinton's new skipper, would run the team from the bench. Completing the arrangements, Germany Schaefer, baseball's reigning clown prince, agreed to handle the duties of public address announcer and to perform his comic routines for the amusement of the crowd.

Even mother nature cooperated. By noontime on game day the skies were clear, calming the organizing committee. A total of $3,049 had been raised by the advance sale of seats. Most of these seats remained empty, because the players and other baseball men who had bought them were either hundreds of miles away or warming up on the playing field.

The gates opened at noon. A delegation of 100, led by Addie's business partner, Abe Holt, arrived from Toledo. The total attendance, including the advance sale, numbered 15,281. Game proceeds were $12,914.60, and pledges collected later pushed the count well over $13,000 for a stunned Lillian Joss.

The visiting stars gathered before the game and posed for one of the game's most fascinating and poignant images. Seven of them squeeze accommodatingly onto five chairs in the front row, where Speaker sags into the space between Schaefer and Crawford. Cobb, squeezed uncomfortably between McAleer and Street, is dressed in a Cleveland uniform because his Detroit flannels had somehow gotten lost. Baby-faced fireballer Wood stands next to fastball king Johnson. The cream of the American League's first decade, brought together by grief and admiration, pauses for a moment on this sad but not somber occasion. Their presence in Cleveland for this benefit game tells us how clearly they understood the precarious economic situation of even the greatest ballplayers, and it also confirms the fondness and respect in which Addie Joss was held by his peers.

The "Joss Game" All Stars.
Back row (l to r): Bobby Wallace, Frank "Home Run" Baker,
Smoky Joe Wood, Walter Johnson, Hal Chase, Clyde Milan,
Russ Ford, Eddie Collins. Front row: Germany Schaefer,
Tris Speaker, Sam Crawford, Jimmy McAleer, Ty Cobb
(in a Cleveland uniform), Gabby Street, Paddy Livingston.

At 2:45, the Cleveland team raced on the field, signaling the long awaited start of the benefit game. The flag in center field flew at half mast, but no flowers or wreaths or black crepe hung about the playing field. This game honored Addie's memory in a joyous, splendid, festival of the sport he loved so dearly.

He pitched good ball, and what he was beside
He did not say, but showed in gentle acts;
No braggart he, nor puffed with empty pride;
A model for his kind in simple facts.
Just what he was he was and never tried
With vain acclaim to be what he was not.

No strength he bragged nor weakness he denied;
The best he had to give was what you got.
An honest tribute this, from one and all:
He pitched good ball

Hugh Keough, Chicago Tribune

Delayed Entry

FORTY YEARS AFTER ADDIE'S DEATH, he was inducted with the first class into the new Wisconsin Sports Hall of Fame, along with Ginger Beaumont, Kid Nichols, and Al Simmons. Still spry at eighty-four, Cy Young represented his friend before a large contingent of Josses and Staudenmayers.

But his relatives had to wait decades for another induction, one that seemed might never occur. Soon after the Baseball Hall of Fame was established in Cooperstown, New York in the late 1930s, a special old-timers committee selected Ed Walsh, Rube Waddell, Eddie Plank, Jack Chesbro, and Jesse Burkett. The committee couldn't select–or even consider–Addie. The rule was clear. Regardless of his accomplishments, a player needed to have played in ten major league seasons to be eligible. Addie had died before being able to take the mound in his tenth. Four twenty-game seasons in a row; two no-hitters (one a perfect game); seven one-hitters; forty-five shutouts in nine years; a lifetime earned run average of 1.88 (second only to Walsh's); the fewest bases on balls allowed per game. None of this mattered any more than his reputation in the first decade of the American League's existence as among his circuit's top pitchers year after year. He simply didn't qualify.

In 1953 a new permanent veterans committee chose Bobby Wallace. Sam Crawford got the nod in 1957. Six years later a surprised and overjoyed Elmer Flick received news of his election. The committee couldn't even consider Addie Joss. An old time New York City semipro manager named George Halpin living in New York put Addie's predicament in focus when he refused to visit Cooperstown. "It isn't the real Hall of Fame if Joss isn't in it," he told the Hall's Ken Smith. "If not the greatest of all pitchers, he is close to it."

But in 1973 the Hall of Fame announced the election of Roberto Clemente, tragically killed in a plane crash the previous year. In doing so the Hall waived the rule that requires a player to be retired from the game for five seasons to be considered for induction. The well-deserved and entirely appropriate waiver did not escape the attention of a cousin of Addie, Dr. Bill Swartz. He began writing letters, and in late 1975 received an encouraging response from Joe Reichler, then special assistant to Commissioner Bowie Kuhn. Reichler wrote, "Your letter urging the election of Addie Joss to the Hall of Fame struck a responding chord here. I have been advocating the same for some time." Reichler said he believed the ten year rule should be relaxed so that the veterans committee could consider Addie for induction.

In August, 1977, Reichler restated his position on the ten year rule when he wrote to Swartz about his appointment to serve on a special review board. He planned to recommend a rule change to allow deserving players such as Addie to become eligible. Two months later, the board changed the rule and allowed exceptions for players whose great careers were shortened by death or illness. Five months later the veterans committee—one of whose members, sportswriter Fred Lieb, had actually seen Addie pitch— met to discuss the merits of a tall, thin pitcher who had last walked the earth sixty-seven years before. On January 30, 1978 the committee elected Addie Joss to the Baseball Hall of Fame.

Addie Joss is a nearly forgotten name as we approach the 100th anniversary of his rookie season. He lived, excelled, and died before Ty Cobb's career was a quarter over, before George Ruth turned pro and became the Babe, before the Snodgrass Muff or the Miracle Braves, before newsreels and radio. He lives for us in the mists of the game's mythological past, in posed pitching images and stiff portraits and vague recollections of distant tragedy. We see him best, not in anecdotes dug out of yellowing newspapers or in the pages of the *Baseball Encyclopedia*, but in the photo taken almost casually on his greatest day in the game, the day when he was perfect. See him sitting easily with his friend Ed Walsh, both men wrapped in wool team sweaters and holding the thick-handled bats of their day. These are two working men. Neither the big, husky Walsh nor the tall, lanky Joss allows two runs in nine innings, and they both know they're in for a rough day on the job. But here they are, for a moment at least, relaxing together on a plain wooden bleacher in front of unfilled chairs in the grandstand behind them, scuffed spikes planted in unmanicured turf. It's an image of the time: sweet but hard, unselfconscious but aware, tough but open. This is the image of Addie Joss, too. And we know that on this day, as on so many others those many years ago, he was the King of Pitchers.

~ Index